Many miss gems searching
for pearls at the bottom of the sea.

CRACKED MIRROR, CLEAR REFLECTION

SHATTER AN ILLUSION
OF PERFECTION

JULIE BARBERA

CONTENTS

Cover photography: nexus 7/shutterstock.com

ISBN: 978-1-7339550-0-3

Because of the dynamic nature of the Internet, any web addresses or links contained in this book may have changed since publication and may no longer be valid.

Inspireu2Action Inc, 2019 - Cracked Mirror, Clear Reflection: Shatter an Illusion of Perfection

1. Religion & Spirituality : Christian Books & Bibles : Christian Living : Personal Growth 2. Religion & Spirituality : Christian Books & Bibles : Christian Living : Professional Growth 3. Christian Books & Bibles : Christian Living : Leadership 4. Religion & Spirituality : Christian Books & Bibles : Christian Living : Self-Help 5. Christian Books & Bibles : Christian Living : Spiritual Growth 6. Religion & Spirituality : Christian Books & Bibles : Christian Living : Inspirational

First Edition

Dedication

This book is dedicated to my sons, Sebastian and Deangelo. Perfect just as you are and wise beyond your years, I am proud to call myself your mom. Both of you are great blessings in my life. You came into this world as miracles, and I know that God has an extraordinary plan for your lives. Whatever you choose to do in life, I support you. Always believe in yourselves and know that Daddy and I are here cheering you on.

A special thank you to my husband, German. Writing this book wouldn't have been possible without your encouragement, love and support. Always remember, there is no storm we can't weather and nothing we can't do with faith and grace. God has proven Himself faithful, and He will continue to honor the promises in His word. We were brought together as a family for such a time as this. And we are always stronger together.

Thank you, Mom and Dad, for all that you do and all that you have done over the years. You are real examples of what it means to demonstrate support and unconditional love. I find peace in knowing that you are always there with my best interests in mind. Dad, a special thank you for your words of wisdom regarding the art of writing. I admire you and hope that this book makes you and Mom proud.

Thank you to my beloved grandma, Anna Lee Knapp. Words can't express how much I appreciate all that you did for me over the years. You were a friend when I felt alone. You lifted me up when I was down. You believed in me when I lacked confidence in myself. Although you didn't walk with me through every chapter in this book, I know you were there. Your footprints are in every story. And I trust that you are smiling down from heaven.

Thank you to my sister, Amy. You are and always have been my inspiration. You demonstrate what it means to follow your heart and live with purpose. Your determination, perseverance and dedication are to be admired. Everyone who is touched by your beautiful presence and music can sense your desire to make a positive impact on the world. Continue to reach for the stars. If anyone can touch them, it's you.

Thank you to my best friend forever, Tammie Campher. Friends come and go. Many stay in our lives for just a season. I am blessed to have found a friendship to last a lifetime. We have grown and changed a lot over the years, yet our bond is as strong as ever. Days, months and miles may separate us, but I know you are just a phone call away.

Last but not least, thank you to my friends and family who have been an essential part of my journey. I pray that this book empowers you to do what you love, love what you do and live with purpose. Most importantly, I pray that it encourages you to be the best version of you.

MY JOURNEY BEGAN WITH A PAINTBRUSH, PEN AND PENCIL.
MY MANUSCRIPT WAS THE TOOL. A STORY WAS WRITTEN IN TIME.
I NEEDED FAITH TO BELIEVE.

Julie Barbera

1 | Eyes to See, Ears to Hear

"Do you have eyes but fail to see,
and ears but fail to hear?"

(Mark 8:18 NIV)

Was I listening to God's voice or was I unable to hear over the noise? Either way, He wanted my attention. I needed to lay some things down for a season. Perhaps then, I would hear more clearly.

My journey began with a paintbrush, pen and pencil. My manuscript was the tool. A story was written in time. I needed faith to believe.

Losing my voice left me like a painter without a paintbrush. Forced into silence, I unwillingly opened my art box and placed the paintbrush of vocal expression inside. I thought to myself, *What will life be like if I can't speak my mind?*

In search of a tool to replace my voice's paintbrush, I found eyes to see and ears to hear. More aware, I noticed a blunt pencil in the box. I turned to God and asked, "Why is this pencil so dull?" He responded, "That is the pencil I have been using to write on your heart. I have had to press hard to get your attention."

I turned to God and asked, "Why is this pencil so dull?" He responded, "That is the pencil I have been using to write on your heart. I have had to press hard to get your attention."

At that moment, I exchanged my paintbrush for a pen. God and I began to write in unison. I had a pen in hand, and He held a dull pencil. But something was different. For the first time in my life, I was listening to my heart.

My paintbrush—my voice—was still favored over other tools. After all, speech allowed me to express my thoughts quickly. But other instruments in my box looked different now, and every one of them had value.

My family and I were set to go to Saint Augustine that weekend. I was unhappy that I couldn't speak. God knew exactly what He was doing. He knew I needed to learn to listen.

While on the trip, my voice slowly returned. I wasn't really anxious for it to come back. In fact, I enjoyed the silence that went along with a muted voice and an open heart.

Able to use my paintbrush once again, I had a newfound appreciation for silence. I went back to my art box to lay my pen down. With hesitation, I exchanged it for my voice.

Suddenly, I noticed something was missing. The blunt pencil was no longer in the box. I turned to God and asked, "What

CRACKED MIRROR, CLEAR REFLECTION

happened to the dull pencil?" His response: "The pencil is now sharp. I no longer have to press hard to get your attention."

Thus began my journey through the simple teaching of a paintbrush, pen and pencil. God imprinted a blueprint on my heart. Life would never be the same.

Every person must lay his or her paintbrush down for a season. This helps us to hear more clearly. Some try to paint their own picture, and dark paint covers the story. Words written on the heart are impossible to read.

Although I tried to listen to God's voice, the noise was all around. The music was so loud that it blocked out the melody. This made it difficult to hear clearly. I couldn't even hear over my own thoughts.

Unwilling to silence my voice, it was taken away for a season. The world somehow looked different. Inspiration was all around, and I needed this experience to see.

My paintbrush was tucked away. God had a sharp pencil in hand, and I held a pen. Together, we would write my story.

Alone at the kitchen table, I looked outside. A butterfly fluttered by and then landed on the ledge right beside my window. Suddenly, I was reminded of the truth. "But blessed are your eyes because they see, and your ears because they hear" (Matthew 13:16 NIV).

EVERY DREAM UNREALIZED IS LIKE A MASTERPIECE NEVER PAINTED,
A HIT SONG NEVER SUNG, A GREAT BOOK NEVER WRITTEN.

EVERY DREAM REALIZED BEGAN WITH A STEP OF FAITH,
A SINGLE ACT OF COURAGE.

Julie Barbera

2 | A Flicker of Light

"You are the light of the world.
A town built on a hill cannot be hidden."

(Matthew 5:14 NIV)

W as I alone or was God there all along? Either way, I wrestled with doubt. Although I had gone through many trials, I had seen miracles. God had proven himself faithful, yet my faith wavered more than I would like to admit.

Lessons needed to be learned. Weaknesses would eventually turn into strengths. My beliefs would be challenged again and again, and the truth would be revealed in time.

It was 2015 when a trip to Saint Augustine opened my eyes. A simple outing to a lighthouse helped me to see. Coincidentally,

I lost my voice a few days prior. Since I was left without a voice, I had no choice but to listen.

As I approached the lighthouse entrance, the front door was ajar. I gently knocked and then poked my head inside. After a moment of silence, I carefully opened the door. The scene quickly reminded me of my past. If for just an instant, I journeyed to another place in time.

With my husband and two young sons by my side, I stood in awe. The grand spiraling staircase was magnificent. The room was dark, and light peeked through tiny windows on every side.

When I was ready to begin my ascent, I stopped for a moment to look up. The view was amazing. The spiraling staircase appeared to be never-ending. It felt like I would never make it to the top. A bright light lit up the ceiling. It stretched from the top of the lighthouse to the entrance floor.

I paused on the second floor to look out a small window. Suddenly, I caught a glimpse of my past. As I thought about lonely days, my future felt uncertain. I was walking with my head down. I looked isolated, but I wasn't alone. There was someone by my side.

The staircase was full of twists and turns. While I had forgotten many experiences, I had securely tucked others away. As challenges came to my mind, I didn't want to think about them. It appeared I had no choice when I was forced to remember.

I stopped to look out the fourth-floor window. I saw myself running. Perhaps I was running from life. The world seemed to be against me. There was sadness in my eyes, but I wasn't without hope. A bright light directed my path.

I continued my ascent and then stopped to pause on the seventh floor. Instantly, I sensed an uncomfortable feeling. I didn't feel good enough to continue my journey. Loneliness followed me through the lighthouse. Insecurity and doubt met me on the seventh floor.

Then I saw myself sitting on a bench. I was reading a book. It appeared I was relaxing, but there was a look of despair in my eyes. Surprisingly, I wasn't friendless. Someone was by my side.

Suddenly, I had a vision. Maybe it was just a dream. Perhaps it would happen in time. Either way, it opened my eyes.

As I thought about my blessings and strengths, I watched. I walked with confidence with my head held high. With a smile on my face, I stepped onto a stage. My book was in hand, and I began to share.

Instantly, the truth was revealed. My story was already written in time. I just needed to trust. Years of doubt suddenly drifted away as I climbed the staircase with ease.

With only two floors left to climb, I was nearing the catwalk. The higher I climbed, the more I could see. With every step forward, the past drifted further and further away from me.

Negativity followed me through the lighthouse. Positivity met me at the top. While I had encountered many obstacles in my life, I was blessed beyond measure.

Although I had felt alone, I was never on my own. God had been by my side every step of the way.

The higher I climbed, the more I could see. With every step forward, the past drifted further and further away from me.

Twists and turns had made the road bumpy. Life's challenges had made my journey difficult. There was a reason for everything, and nothing would go to waste.

Towering above the ocean, I proudly stood on the catwalk. I watched as ships passed. The light at the top was brighter than ever. I wanted to share with my family, but my voice was still silenced. They had no idea what had just played out in my mind. Perhaps they were busy creating their own story.

My speech would soon return. Saddened, I promised myself that I would maintain an open heart. Silence speaks to the soul. A muted voice allows inspiration to speak. My experience would eventually make it to paper. And it would soon become a part of my story.

God's grace was all around. At that moment, I realized I was blessed. I just needed help to see. Suddenly, a still small voice called from the lantern room. "For I know the plans I have for you," declares the Lord, "plans to prosper you and not to harm you, plans to give you hope and a future" (Jeremiah 29:11 NIV).

A MIRROR REFLECTS WHAT'S INSIDE.
WORDS ECHO WHAT'S IN THE HEART.
YOUR LIGHT CAN SHINE BRIGHTLY, EVEN THROUGH THE CRACKS.

DOUBT SEES FLAWS AND WEAKNESSES.
HOPE SEES BLESSINGS AND STRENGTHS.
A SIMPLE REFLECTION CHANGES EVERYTHING.

Julie Barbera

3 | Imprints Unseen

"There you saw how the Lord your God carried you,
as a father carries his son, all the way you went
until you reached this place."

(Deuteronomy 1:31 NIV)

W as there one set of footprints or were there two? Either
way, I decided to follow them. I set out on a journey, and
imprints in the sand led the way. I wondered if I would see things
missed or realize things misunderstood. Perhaps I would wish life
had been lived differently.

Memories of a trip to Saint Augustine were fresh in mind.
My family and I had just returned, and I arrived with a

newfound appreciation for silence. Inspiration finally had a voice. It spoke through the simplest of things.

It was early morning. As was my daily routine, I sat at the kitchen table alone. This was my time to think. The silence made it possible to hear God's voice. Although I was fully present, my mind drifted to another place in time. With a cup of coffee in hand, I picked up my pen to write.

What started as an ordinary day turned into a day like no other. Footprints led to a pretty, pink seashell. I picked up the shell and then placed it over my ear. As expected, sounds were trapped inside. They weren't relaxing, and they certainly didn't come from the ocean.

Suddenly, I had a vision. The scene was all too familiar. I watched as a child quietly snuck out the front door. Yelling rang out into the streets, and it could be heard blocks away. I quickly realized I was watching myself at the young age of ten.

With my ears covered, I went up a steep hill. I ran alone in the dark. Although I was scared, I had done this many times before. Grandma's house was just a block away. I knew it would be peaceful there. It always was.

When I spotted a pier in the distance, I followed imprints in the sand. They led to the water's edge. I looked down and saw a reflection in the water. It took a moment to make out the image. I soon realized I was watching my fifteen-year-old self.

As I stood in front of the mirror, I gazed at my reflection. Since I was unhappy with what I saw, I stepped on the scale. I did this several times a day with the hope that the number would change.

The scale was my gauge. It was used to measure self-worth. Excessive exercise and a strict diet gave me a sense of control. Aside from that, life felt completely out of control.

All of a sudden, the front door opened. It was dark and bitter cold outside. Snow covered the ground. Although it was difficult to make out a clear path ahead, I had to run. This was my routine.

I walked a few steps and then quickly picked up the pace. I made my way to the North High running track. Once I was there, I ran alone in the dark for miles. I suppose I was running from life.

The sun began to rise. This reminded me that I was almost done with my daily regimen. Since my mission was accomplished, I made my way back home. Grandma knew I had left early that morning. As usual, she met me at the front door with a smile.

Although I was exhausted, I returned with a feeling of completion. Once my exercise was done for the day, nothing else really mattered. I simply had to control my diet.

Despite my imperfections, Grandma accepted me unconditionally. I am sure she saw my flaws, yet she made no mention of them. I looked down and noticed one set of footprints, but I now realize that there were two. God kept Grandma in my life to carry me through.

The scene changed drastically. I was at Salisbury State University in a college dorm room. I still struggled with low self-esteem and an eating disorder, only now I was overeating. Food was used for comfort. Fear of gaining weight had pushed me in the opposite direction.

College life was difficult. Frankly, I wasn't ready to break old habits. It was even more challenging without Grandma by my side.

As I watched intently, a car pulled up in front of my dormitory. Since I was ready to go with my bags packed, I got inside. Then the car pulled away. I had to leave college life behind to start counseling for a compulsive overeating problem. I went back to my hometown in Hagerstown, and I would finish my first two years at Hagerstown Junior College.

The setting quickly changed. I was sitting in a waiting room. A kind counselor walked out to greet me. I had my doubts, but I had no choice. I needed to get help. He reassured me I would get better. It was time to work through issues, and it would take years to recover.

Once the session was over, I walked out of the office with my head down. Then I noticed several sets of footprints. While I felt alone, I didn't walk alone. God put the counselor in my path. Mom, Dad and Grandma also helped me through this trying time in my life.

When I noticed a large object in the distance, I followed imprints in the sand. I was eighteen years old, and I had found a treasure chest. The scene quickly changed, and I was sitting in the back of a small, country church. A pastor was preaching. I was alone, and I was the only person in the pew.

The pastor asked those who didn't know Christ to come forward. Nobody responded. My heart was pounding. I didn't want to be the only person standing, so I held back the urge to raise my hand. Then he spoke up again, and my hand went up. I had no idea what had just happened. I didn't even know why I was there.

My hands were shaking as I walked to the front of the church. I stopped in the middle of the aisle, and the pastor prayed a quick prayer for my salvation. Although I didn't fully understand what was going on, I sensed a change. I lacked self-confidence, so it was hard to believe that God would step down from heaven to meet me.

The service ended. I got up and quietly walked out of the building. As I looked down, I noticed two sets of footprints. Little did I know, I would never feel lonely again. I was forever changed, and my life would never be the same.

Many times, I saw one set of footprints. Other times, I saw two. At times, there were many. One thing was sure: I was never alone.

We walk this path solo, yet God is always by our side. He

brings angels into our lives. They walk the earth just like you and me. We don't necessarily see it at the time. It's evident later. We look back and realize that we actually walked with angels in disguise.

Yes, I saw things missed. Many things were misunderstood. Negative wasn't really negative at all. In reality, it was all good. I didn't wish life had been lived differently. Good and bad, I understood the reason for struggle and pain.

We look back and realize that we actually walked with angels in disguise.

Every experience was a blessing. Everything happened for a reason. Some reasons were visible, and others were much harder to see. Yet, I was thankful for every experience. It was all part of becoming a better me.

I turned to follow another trail. I looked down, and words of hope were written in the sand. "Your path led through the sea, your way through the mighty waters, though your footprints were not seen" (Psalm 77:19 NIV).

DON'T LET SHORTFALLS DEFINE YOU.
SEE STRUGGLE AS YOUR GREATEST TEACHER.
LET CHALLENGES BUILD TRUE STRENGTH.

YOU'RE STRONGER THAN YOUR CIRCUMSTANCES.
EVERY EXPERIENCE HAS VALUE.
USE IT TO MAKE A DIFFERENCE.

Julie Barbera

4 | Storm's Reflection

"God is our refuge and strength,
an ever-present help in trouble."

(Psalm 46:1 NIV)

Would storms overwhelm me or would strength come after every storm? Either way, rainy days were a part of life. I had experienced my fair share. I longed for sunnier days yet held on to hope. Perhaps I needed both highs and lows to grow.

Challenges turned into lessons, and the struggle became my story. Many chapters were still unfinished. Although written in time, my narrative was far from complete.

It was early morning. I sat on the balcony alone. At a loss for words, it was challenging to write. Silence allowed inspiration to speak, and this was my time to listen.

With a cup of coffee in hand, my story picked up where it left off days prior. Reflecting on the past had somehow made it easier to move forward. Although I had overcome many challenges, life had made the triumphs easy to forget. Surprisingly, I had over-looked an important part of my story.

Footprints led to a viewing station. I spotted a boat in the distance with a young woman inside. A storm was developing. Clouds began to form as the vehicle entered rough waters. I looked closely and realized I was watching myself.

Inspired, I picked up my pen and scribbled words on a crumbled up piece of paper. *If you are ready to give up, don't give in. Reflect on how far you have come. You will find the courage to start again.*

If you are ready to give up, don't give in. Reflect on how far you have come. You will find the courage to start again.

Suddenly, the story played out. I was twenty-four years old, and I had just finished my daily workout at Gold's Gym in Sunrise, Florida. Since I was ready to leave the gym, I went to the locker room to gather my belongings. As I walked past a mirror, I caught a glimpse of my reflection. I paused for just a moment and thought to myself: *Why are you so focused on what you see in the mirror? You are never satisfied, and nothing is good enough. Life has to be more than this.*

After years of battling with an eating disorder, I had come a long way. Still, I was too focused on the superficial. My identity was my physical appearance. A constant pursuit for perfection controlled me.

In a hurry, I made my way to the front door. I am not sure

what I was rushing to do, but I was always rushing to do something.

As I was ready to leave the parking lot, I looked in the rearview mirror. While I was outwardly humble, I struggled with pride. Realizing this prompted me to pray. "Lord, please humble me." Little did I know, I was in the calm before the storm.

What started as a simple prayer would turn into a big lesson. I had no idea how God would answer my prayer. I certainly didn't think it would affect the next four years of my life. I quickly dismissed the thought and went back to my daily business.

The next morning, I woke up with a big surprise. My face had broken out. I had never experienced problems with break-outs. While odd, this didn't seem like a big deal at the time.

Days went by, and my face didn't clear up as expected. I developed ulcers in my mouth. I started to notice dark spots on my face. My monthly cycle abruptly stopped, and other symptoms began to pile up.

Stress was more than likely the culprit. I was sure my health issues would resolve. In an attempt to turn things around, I quickly made lifestyle changes. When my symptoms didn't subside, distress set in. The calm had ended, and I was in the midst of the storm.

A tiring battle to find answers had begun. With determination, I went from doctor to doctor. None acknowledged my issue as real. Most told me the problem was all in my head. My symptoms were undoubtedly genuine, and there had to be an answer.

Since I was frustrated, I shared my story with anyone who would listen. I was working as a personal trainer at the time. A couple of my clients had suggested that I look for a gynecological endocrinologist. I felt that I had exhausted my efforts to get help, and I had mostly given up on conventional medicine.

On my way home from college one evening, I cried out,

"God, I need help. Please put someone in my life who will listen and believe me. I need answers."

That day at college was more difficult than most. I struggled to make it through my last class. I felt hot, and then I began to sweat excessively. Embarrassment prompted me to leave in the middle of class. I dealt with these symptoms every week, only other weeks I was able to stick it out.

It was 6 a.m. the following morning. I was in the gym waiting for my 7 a.m. personal training appointment. My 6 a.m. had canceled at the last minute.

While I waited for my next session, I overheard a man say he was a doctor. Curious, I asked, "Sir, did you say you are a doctor?" He responded, "Yes, I am a gynecological endocrinologist." My heart began to beat rapidly. Maybe God had answered my cry for help. *Was this my answer?*

After sharing my story, the kind doctor offered to help. I had no insurance at the time. I had to pay for medical tests, but he would provide his services for free. My family agreed to cover the cost of testing.

When I looked down, I was reminded of the truth. Several sets of footprints were lined up side by side. While I felt lonely, I wasn't alone. God put others in my path to help me through the storm.

After extensive testing to confirm that my problem wasn't related to nutrition or something within my control, I was given a diagnosis. At the young age of twenty-seven, I was entering menopause. The doctor said that my only solutions were estrogen replacement therapy and in vitro fertilization. Deeply saddened by this news, I left the doctor's office in tears.

Premature menopause meant I would never be able to have children. I could try in vitro fertilization, but I wasn't ready to have children. I wasn't married. I wasn't even in a relationship, and I certainly didn't have the money to pay for the expensive treatment. Low estrogen meant future health issues. The doctor stated that reversal was highly unlikely, and I needed to act fast.

Although I was discouraged, I refused to accept such a fate. After a four-year battle with fear, I chose to walk in faith. I began to read scriptures on healing. Almost ready to give up, I held on to a glimmer of hope. I was praying for a miracle.

My sister had introduced me to a pastor friend a few months prior. He suddenly began to call daily. At times, he called me several times a day. Uncomfortable with the frequency of his calls, I chose not to answer.

Weeks went by, and the calls continued. One day the phone rang. Something felt different that day. For whatever reason, I decided to answer.

After speaking with the pastor for a few minutes, the reason for his calls was apparent. I was praying for healing. He had the gift of healing, and God had prompted him to call.

He had no idea that I had been struggling with health issues. He was unaware that I had been praying for a miracle. I shared my story and then asked for prayer. I was insistent. I bowed my head as he began to pray. I didn't say much, but I held on to hope. Although the prayer was quick, I sensed a change immediately.

Despite a lack of physical evidence, something felt different. A few days later, my symptoms of premature menopause began to reverse. My monthly cycle returned, and I never went back for further testing. I had my doubts, but I held on to hope. I believed by faith.

I looked down. Two sets of footprints were lined up side by side. I hadn't walked through the storm alone. God was with me; He was always by my side.

Two years later, I met my husband, German. We were blessed with two wonderful sons, Sebastian and Deangelo. All happened by the grace of God.

Although the storm felt over-whelming, it didn't overpower me. It changed me. Valuable lessons were learned. A simple prayer for humility not only humbled me, but it also built courage and strength.

Storms would follow in the years to come. It was a challenge to go through them, but I had learned to trust by faith. This experience taught me a valuable lesson. No matter how difficult the situation, never, ever lose hope.

> Storms would follow in the years to come. It was a challenge to go through them, but I had learned to trust by faith.

Inspired by the story, the storm's reflection was clear. The sun had come up, and I heard voices coming from inside the house. My family had woken up.

It was time to put my pen and paper away for the day. I thoughtfully wrote down words of hope. "He stilled the storm to a whisper; the waves of the sea were hushed" (Psalm 107:29 NIV).

STRENGTH COMES AFTER EVERY STORM.
DURING THE HEAVIEST OF DOWNPOURS,
WE MUST LEARN TO DANCE IN THE RAIN.

RAIN GIVES LIFE. RAINY DAYS REMIND US THAT WE'RE ALIVE.
WE NEED BOTH RAIN AND SUN TO GROW.

Julie Barbera

5 | Glimmer of Hope

"Now faith is the substance of things hoped for,
the evidence of things not seen."

(Hebrews 11:1 NKJV)

W as I ready to take a chance or was it best to wait? Either
came with risk. If I took a step, I might fail or make a
mistake. I could stand still, but the vision would never come to
pass if I played it safe.

Life was full of cloudy skies yet mixed with sunny days.
Storms made me stronger. While brighter days lifted my spirits,
complacency tried to sneak in. Every experience taught valuable
lessons.

Bad weather was temporary. Complacency needed to be

overcome. A desire to change needed to be stronger than fear of change. Then I would find the courage to take a step.

With a pen in hand, it was time to write. I scribbled words on a piece of paper. Inspiration didn't come, so I stopped to read the Bible. I needed courage for the journey ahead, and faith gave me direction.

All of a sudden, I had a vision of myself at thirty-four. I was standing along the shore. A boat had just arrived, and passengers were boarding. I wanted to step on, but I was too afraid to board. A look of loneliness was on my face, but I wasn't alone. My husband and young son were by my side. Another baby was on the way.

A desire to change needed to be stronger than fear of change. Then I would find the courage to take a step.

Although I had seen a lot in my life, many things were still hard to understand. Much of what I had experienced made me stronger and increased my faith. The family by my side was my greatest miracle, yet something was missing.

As I was drawn into the scene, my mind drifted to another place in time. If for just an instant, my dream came to mind. What started as a big vision faded to a flicker of hope. The vision kept the dream alive. The light was always on, and nothing could put it out.

God had healed me of premature menopause a few years prior. Pregnant with my second son, I was dealing with a blood condition known as thrombocytopenia. Low platelets made the pregnancy risky. I couldn't understand why God would heal me and then allow this to happen.

My platelets stayed low throughout the pregnancy. At times, they went up slightly and then dropped back down. I was concerned about the C-section, as my doctors had warned me of the risks.

Every challenge comes with a silver lining. Many that crossed my path would hear my story. I viewed this as an opportunity to share my testimony of healing, and my pregnancy was irrefutable evidence.

While I was afraid of the risks and concerned about the consequences, I held on to hope. Despite my fear and doubt, I openly declared that God would show up. Some believed with hesitation, while others completely disagreed. One doctor believed wholeheartedly.

The big day finally arrived. My husband and I were on our way to the hospital. I was excited yet very concerned at the same time. Words of faith had been spoken throughout my pregnancy, and I was ready to see my miracle.

We prayed before leaving the house. Although I was silent, a million thoughts went through my mind. I wrestled with fear and doubt, but one thing that stuck was a number. I thought to myself, *Thank you, Lord, that my platelets are 130,000.*

A STAT test two days prior had come back with a platelet count below half of that number. Another test needed to be done before the C-section. The results would determine the direction for the delivery.

While at the hospital, I awaited the big moment. A lab technician frantically rushed in to draw my blood. Oddly, they had forgotten about the STAT test. I heard the concern in their voices as all waited for the results. My doctor hadn't arrived yet, and he needed to give direction for the surgery.

God had shown up numerous times in the past. Miracles are something you never forget. Although I was afraid, my faith was strong. Doubt tried to sneak in, but hope seemed to win.

Suddenly, a lab technician showed up at the door. She looked shocked as she yelled out the results, "Her platelet count is 130,000." Disbelief filled the room as all began to speak at once.

"That isn't possible. A platelet count doesn't change that quickly. There must be a mistake."

Medical staff spoke amongst themselves. I shared my testimony with the anesthesiology nurse, as she was the one person in the room who believed me. Then I spoke up loud enough for all to hear. "Yes, it is possible. With God, all things are possible."

When the delivering doctor arrived, the anesthesiologist quickly spoke up. "Doctor, her platelet count came back at 130,000, and we know this isn't possible. A platelet count doesn't change that quickly without medication. What do you want to do?"

My doctor confidently stated, "Proceed as planned. She told me this would happen." At that moment, I realized that I was witnessing my miracle.

The scene changed unexpectedly. Once again, I was standing along the shore. I glanced down and noticed a set of footprints. I was reminded that God had carried me through the storm.

Another boat was ready to dock. I could see it in the distance. I had missed many opportunities in the past, and this was my chance.

Ready to board, I looked down at the water below. The boat captain looked me straight in the eye and said, "Ma'am, would you like to board?" I didn't want to answer. There was a possibility that doubt would prompt me to turn back. Finally, I built up the courage to take a step.

Time on the boat allowed me to reflect. Life's heavy burdens made my dreams seem impossible. A thankful heart was crushed under worries of the world. Daily responsibilities were weighing me down. Despite my circumstances, I resolved to move forward.

When we were almost to shore, the boat captain prepared all for arrival. I was nervous yet ready. Then the captain looked my way and signaled for me to exit. One foot in front of the other, I made my way to the exit ramp. Ready to step off, I looked down at the water below.

Suddenly, I saw my reflection. I wasn't ready. I had a big vision, but the timing wasn't right. I quietly muttered the words, "One day, not today. When things are better, then I will pursue my dream."

That day was my day. I took one step forward. There was no more waiting, and time was passing me by. Afraid yet ready, I stepped off the boat into the unknown of the other side.

Although I still faced challenges, they had lost the power to

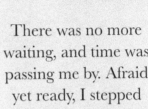

There was no more waiting, and time was passing me by. Afraid yet ready, I stepped off the boat into the unknown of the other side.

hold me back. Life involved risk. I was nervous, and there was a possibility I would fail. Regardless, I found the courage to take a step.

I laid my pen down and then turned to look out the balcony window. Words of hope gave me the strength to continue. "For I know the plans I have for you," declares the Lord, "plans to prosper you and not to harm you, plans to give you hope and a future" (Jeremiah 29:11 NIV).

HOPE IS A TINY SPARK THAT
MAKES A BIG DIFFERENCE.
THE LIGHT MAY GROW DIM,
BUT IT NEVER GOES OUT.

Julie Barbera

6 | Looking Glass

"And we know that in all things God works
for the good of those who love him,
who have been called according to his purpose."

(Romans 8:28 NIV)

Did everything happen for a reason or was life just a series of random events? Either way, I resolved to find meaning. Sometimes the purpose was clear, and other times it was hard to see. Maybe one day all would make sense.

Seeds of hope were planted, and I tried to water them. At times, they grew. Most of the time, weeds of worry sprung up to choke the vision. Doubt was there. Fear tried to stop me. Faith always seemed to win.

It was early morning. I sat at the table alone. With my Bible open, I sought answers to life's most difficult questions. Faith as a guide, I continued to write my story.

One foot was still in the boat, and I had just set foot on the other side. Footprints were imprinted in the soil below my feet. Although I was apprehensive about the journey ahead, I decided to follow them.

Questions arose. *If I were able to alter my reflection, would I? If it were possible to change the past, would I have lived differently?* Answers didn't come quickly. After all, it had taken years to build up the courage to step out.

The other side was different than I imagined. My vision was the same, but the way I perceived it had changed. It was still big, yet it somehow seemed smaller. Perhaps it was I who was standing just a little taller.

Turning back didn't even seem like an option anymore. I had finally stepped into my moment: that instant when one's destiny is shaped. I could turn back, but I had gone too far.

As I approached a beautiful tower, footprints led the way. The door was large and plated with gold. A high pillar stretched to the heavens. It appeared as if it had stood the test of time.

Since I was hesitant to knock, I walked around the corner. The tower was covered with stained glass windows. Every window told a story. Many scenes were mysteriously familiar, while other memories were seemingly forgotten.

Greeted by a young woman, she welcomed me inside. Her

resemblance to me was striking. A man and two young boys stood by her side.

The entrance looked like a museum. A large book was propped up on a podium to the right of the door. I had to sign in before taking a tour.

Stained glass windows covered the walls. Every window reflected a moment in time: a reflection from the past. Together, they told my story.

Suddenly, the scene changed. I was standing in a health club with a young girl. She had just finished a workout session, and I was her personal trainer. Healthy habits had turned into an unhealthy mindset. My client was struggling and needed help. I listened attentively, and my goal was to plant seeds of hope.

I moved to another window, and the scene quickly changed. I was still in the gym but with an older woman. Her story was different. She struggled with confidence, and I was there to listen.

Many crossed my path. Some came into my life for a moment in time. Others stuck around for several seasons. Whatever the case, I seized the moment. My mission was to encourage and spread hope. Although I was just a trainer, I sensed a higher calling.

Inspired, I began my ascent up a large iron staircase. Memories covered the wall. Moment by moment flashed before my eyes. Then I realized an essential part of my story was missing.

The past tried to steal my future. I struggled with low self-esteem, compulsive overexercising and overeating. These remnants from yesterday would stay on the second floor. The lessons learned would serve as a reminder.

My early years were less than ideal. I experienced my fair share of trials. While I went through many challenges, they had prepared me for such a time as this. The past wasn't the focus, yet it would inspire me to make a difference in the future.

Encouraged by the second floor, I continued my journey up

the spiraling staircase. I arrived on the third floor and then made my way around a circular room. One scene caught my attention.

It was a Wednesday. I had somehow forgotten about Wednesdays. That was my day to be. I would pray, "God, lead me. Take me wherever you want me to be. Put the right people in my path." *I learned a lot about life on Wednesdays.*

As I sat alone in a coffee shop, I was reading the newspaper. I knew almost everyone who walked through the door. Seemingly engaged in what I was doing, I waited for the right moment.

At times, I walked in and randomly sat with a stranger. Of course, I only did this when prompted. Other times, I sat alone. God never ceased to amaze me. Either I needed to be encouraged, or the other person needed encouragement. *I learned a lot about promptings from God at the coffee shop.*

As I looked across the room, I spotted a woman seated at a corner table. Since I noticed distress in her eyes, I invited her to join me. She began to share her story. Sadly, she had woken up feeling very depressed. In desperate need of encouragement, she had mustered up the strength to leave her house that morning.

The woman's prayer was that God would send someone to help. I had also prayed a prayer that morning. I asked God to put someone in my path to encourage. The woman somehow ended up at my table at the coffee shop.

God was faithful every day, and nothing happened by chance. I experienced countless moments like these, especially on Wednesdays. Many others like the woman crossed my path, men and women, both young and old. Opportunities to plant seeds of hope were all around. I just needed to find them.

Although I was just a young woman, I sensed a higher purpose. My confidence was shaky, but that didn't stop me. I was sure that my experiences would be used to help others and make a difference.

Inspired to go higher, I climbed the iron staircase. The fourth floor looked empty. Then I realized I had stepped into a large auditorium. The podium was center stage, and chairs were lined up side by side.

The stage reminded me of my sister, Amy. She had sung in the church for years. In pursuit of her dream, she sang at numerous events. All admired her beautiful voice. I was happy for her, but I felt a little left out. I had talents but not the kind others noticed. I had dreams but nothing substantial.

Suddenly, I spotted two young women seated in the front row. I walked within earshot to listen. One woman was me, and the other was my sister. She had forgotten to share a prophetic word that was given to her a few days prior. Something prompted her to share at that moment.

After singing at a church event, Amy was approached by the sound technician. He had a prophetic word to share regarding her music. An unexpected word was given about me. The man said, "One day God is going to do amazing things in your sister's life. She is going to speak in front of thousands in many languages."

This word sounded pleasant to my ear, yet there seemed to be no truth to the message. I greatly feared public speaking. I had no interest at all in learning another language, let alone many. So, I quickly shrugged off my sister's words.

Despite what I chose to believe, a seed was planted. A word I blew off in an instant turned into a word I would never forget.

No matter how far I drifted, the prophetic word was in the back of my mind. Hope was a tiny spark that made a big difference. The light grew dim, but it never went out. Despite what I chose to believe, a seed was planted. A word I blew off in an instant turned into a word I would never forget.

Yes, everything happened for a reason. At times events

seemed random, but there was always a purpose. And life had prepared me for such a time as this.

My pen would only take me as far as my mind could imagine. That is how it was with dreams. One day they would become a reality. Then and only then would all become clear.

The sun came up. It was time to set my pen down for the day. I quickly glanced at my Bible, and a word from God gave me hope. "For now we see only a reflection as in a mirror; then we shall see face to face. Now I know in part; then I shall know fully, even as I am fully known" (1 Corinthians 13:12 NIV).

———————

**EVERYTHING IN LIFE HAPPENS FOR A REASON.
GOOD AND BAD, IT PREPARES YOU FOR SOMETHING MORE.
ALWAYS A LESSON TO LEARN, IT'S ALL PART OF A GREATER PLAN.**

———————

Julie Barbera

7 | The Vision Awaits

"Write the vision. And make *it* plain on tablets,
that he may run who reads it."

(Habakkuk 2:2 NKJV)

Was my vision of speaking publicly just a dream or would it become a reality? Either way, I held on to hope. A seed was planted. Remnants took root, and portions fell away. Perhaps my full vision would come to pass one day.

Dreams were locked away in my heart. While I struggled to find the right key, I needed to unlock the potential inside. It was there yet so very hard to see.

It took years to build courage, but I finally had direction. My manuscript was the first step. Writing daily was my plan of action. I knew what I wanted to write and how quickly I wanted to write it.

It was soon evident that God was leading. A path was laid out, and inspiration was my guide. Ideas came but not as fast as anticipated. Although years of waiting had finally resulted in action, I still had to wait to put my thoughts on paper.

The hardest part of the journey was reliving the past. I had to go back to move forward, but I couldn't stay there. I had to leave the past in the past. I would carry memories and pack up lessons. I couldn't forget to bring courage, as I needed it to step into the vision.

Memories were powerful. They either limited or inspired me. Whatever the case, I had to come to terms with them. Once dealt with, it was easier to look past challenges. This made possibilities easier to see.

At times, I was confident in my abilities. A majority of the time, I fell short of my expectations. While I had come a long way, I still had a long way to go. My vision was far from reality.

Suddenly, the story picked up where it left off days prior. The past had affected the beginning of my journey. I wouldn't allow it to impact the present, and it wasn't going to limit me. In fact, it had prepared me for such a time as this.

For years, I held on to a vision. I had very little evidence that it would come to pass. Even so, I shared it with others. Hope kept the vision alive. The light was always on. Nothing could put it out. Inspired, I picked up my pen to write.

Hope kept the vision alive. The light was always on. Nothing could put it out.

The prophetic word was clear. *One day God would do amazing things in my life. I would speak in front of thousands in different languages.* This was the vision. How it would play out was yet to be determined.

Memories on the fourth floor inspired me to go higher. They reminded me of my purpose. I walked around the room one last time and then continued my ascent up the winding staircase.

On my way to the fifth floor, I glimpsed at forgotten memories. They lined the walls. Some were from childhood, others young adulthood. They took place anywhere from the coffee shop to the gym. Some were in a classroom, but many were random.

Every story had one thing in common. No matter how difficult the challenge, the end result was positive. Everything happened for a reason. Courage always seemed to win.

I started my journey with negative memories. They were still there, but something had changed. They had somehow lost the power to control me. An ability to look past negative had made positive easier to see.

My search for a higher purpose was never-ending. I held on tight to unbroken dreams. At times, I felt unworthy of the vision. But I learned I didn't need to feel worthy to be worthy. Other times, I felt useless. Yet, I realized I didn't need to feel useful to be used.

Many truths were revealed through an open heart and a ready pen. One simple yet powerful fact was the importance of writing the vision down. Once on paper, it came to life. The truth was the truth. It didn't matter how I felt.

Everything came together on the fifth floor. It was set up like a classroom. I quickly scanned the room. Seated in the back with my hand raised, I spotted myself at twenty-five years old.

I remember that day like it was yesterday. My last semester was almost over. I was on my way to class. In the car alone, God spoke to my heart. "Today you are going to speak. This is your chance."

I was a little late for class that day, so I discreetly snuck in and took my seat. Distracted, I quickly forgot the message.

Suddenly, the teacher made an announcement. "Today we are going to do things differently. Normally I speak. Today a few of you will get the opportunity to speak." I knew what this meant. The message in the car came to mind, and this was my opportunity.

The teacher continued, "Students will be broken into groups of ten. I will pass out a piece of paper for each group. The topics will be discussed, and then all will come to a joint resolution regarding the answers. One person from each group will act as a representative. We have twelve groups. We will have time for just a few to speak."

Everyone waited patiently as the teacher passed out the topics. I joined forces with students nearby. When we got our questions, everyone in the group was surprised. Ours were very different from those that others had received.

The subject was pre-nursing. All of the topics were connected to nursing care with one exception: ours. The questions we received had nothing to do with nursing, at least in the literal sense. They were related to the meaning of life, the search for purpose and how we are supposed to treat others.

As a group, we made our way to the outside corridor to discuss. There was one in the group who was an atheist. I was an outspoken Christian. Others were neutral in their beliefs.

A few students quickly spoke up. They felt that the atheist and I would be too strong in our views. It was clear that neither of us should speak. Regardless, I knew what I was supposed to do.

The class was almost over, and I could hear the teacher from outside. He announced that there was time for one last speaker. I didn't want to miss my chance, so I prompted the group to go inside.

We had scribbled a few notes on a piece of paper. We hadn't

come to a resolution nor had we designated a speaker for the group. We had only come to an agreement as to who shouldn't speak.

The teacher spoke up one last time. "Class, I have time for one more speaker." I quickly raised my hand. Students from the group said, "Julie, what are you doing? You know you are not supposed to speak. We didn't even come to an agreement about the answers."

Vision in sight, this was my chance. Then the teacher called my name. Since I wanted confirmation of words spoken years prior, I walked forward.

In front of a packed classroom, I spoke with confidence. I didn't have a paper in hand. I merely spoke from my heart. I shared my perspective on hope, vision and purpose. Students were inspired, and some even came forward to thank me for the encouragement.

All of a sudden, the teacher spoke up and questioned me in front of the class. He asked, "Why are you here?" Shocked, I didn't know how to respond. Then he stated, "You don't belong in nursing. You should be doing this: public speaking."

I quietly walked back to my seat to gather my belongings. Surprisingly, I was greeted by my atheist friend. He stated, "Great job, Julie. I don't know how you did that, but you did. You shared a balanced message of hope. I couldn't have said it better myself."

God was faithful. He didn't leave me to wonder. Instead, He gave me no reason to doubt. I held on to that moment for years. Although short-lived, it gave me hope. And I received confirmation of my calling that day.

When I was ready to go to the next floor, my attention shifted back to the tour. Images on the wall reminded me of the big picture. For years, I was only focused on big dreams. I had somehow forgotten about small things.

At that moment, I came to a realization. I couldn't just

discredit small things that had happened in my life. I needed to write them down. The vision was clear. I needed to put it on paper and keep it in sight.

Although my vision felt like a dream at times, I was confident that it would one day become a reality. Hope kept it alive. And faith gave me the courage to believe that my vision would turn into more than just a dream.

And faith gave me the courage to believe that my vision would turn into more than just a dream.

Since it was time to move forward, I continued my ascent up the spiraling staircase. Words of hope were written on the wall. "For the vision *is* yet for an appointed time; But at the end it will speak, and it will not lie. Though it tarries, wait for it; Because it will surely come, It will not tarry" (Habakkuk 2:3 NKJV).

HAVE BIG DREAMS, BUT BE FAITHFUL IN SMALL THINGS.
IT'S THOSE SMALL THINGS THAT PREPARE YOU FOR THE BIG DREAM.

PLANT SEEDS. BE PATIENT IF RESULTS ARE SLOW.
WATER THEM. IT TAKES TIME FOR DREAMS TO GROW.

Julie Barbera

8 | A Shadow in the Dark

"For everyone to whom much is given,
from him much will be required;
and to whom much has been committed,
of him they will ask the more."

(Luke 12:48 NKJV)

W as the shadow a reflection of what was to come or a way to escape the past? Either way, it kept the vision alive. It seemed more comfortable to settle, but I sensed a greater purpose. I had been given much and with that came much commitment.

A vision was in the back of my mind. Most of the time, it was buried under the heaviness of life's burdens. Still, the light never went out. Small glimpses of hope foreshadowed what was to come.

As was my routine, I woke up to write. The early morning hours allowed for deeper reflection, and dark brought the truth to light. Although I was tempted to give up, I wasn't willing to give in. Some mornings were more difficult than others, and this was one of those days.

Life's noise had drowned out the vision, but I found hope for tomorrow on the fifth floor. Beautiful memories had been forgotten. To build the courage to move forward, I needed to look back long enough to reflect. With my pen in hand, I began to write.

My mind drifted back to the tour. As I continued my ascent up the spiraling staircase, I arrived on the sixth floor. Words written in different languages covered the walls. An illustration beside each caption told a story. Images were positive, but doubt tried to creep in. Hope was in the background, and faith always seemed to win. I was in every scene twice.

> Images were positive, but doubt tried to creep in. Hope was in the background, and faith always seemed to win.

Inspired, a thought came to mind. *One day God will do amazing things in your life. You will speak in front of thousands in different languages.* This was the prophetic word given years prior. I believed but lacked the faith to act on my belief. The message hadn't made it to my heart yet.

Standing in front of the first scene, the story played out. I had just graduated from Florida Atlantic University. In an attempt to find my way in the world, I accepted an entry-level sales position selling spa coupons in the streets. It was anything but glamorous. Surprisingly, God used that simple job to bring my vision to life. I didn't see it at the time, but I would realize years later.

Although short-lived, I worked in Miami for a week. Everyone in the area spoke Spanish. While I only knew a few words, I made an effort to communicate. I formed broken sentences and used the little Spanish that I knew to get my message across.

Suddenly, the scene changed. I was driving to the Lord's Gym in Tamarac, Florida when a phrase in Spanish came to mind. I quickly stopped my car along the side of the road and then jotted down words to form a sentence. Since I was anxious to check my work, I kept the paper nearby.

With the paper in hand, I approached a Spanish speaking friend in the gym. To my surprise, I had written the sentence correctly. Other than the basics required to graduate, I hadn't really studied. In fact, I barely passed the final exam. It seemed that God had given me insight. If for just an instant, my vision came to life.

Thus began my language journey. Since God had implanted a natural desire within me, these events sparked an endless cycle of learning. Once I had started, nothing could stop me. An ability to speak other languages became my shadow in the dark: a reflection of what was to come.

A desire to learn didn't decrease with time. Instead, it increased. I went from Spanish to Portuguese, and then to Italian. At times I forgot about the prophetic word, but it was always in the back of my mind. After all, the languages were tangible evidence.

Life changed over time. I met my husband, and we had two children. The vision was still there, but the stress of everyday life had made it hard to see.

Years went by, and my aspirations were on hold. I didn't have the energy to pursue anything else. And I began to wonder if my vision was nothing more than just an empty dream.

We purchased a house in the Orlando area during the housing bubble. The value of our home had drastically dropped in a matter of months. Moving back to South Florida was necessary, but it was impossible to sell our house at the current market value. In need of direction, my husband and I found a church in Orlando and began to attend a financial freedom class. Since we felt more judgment than support from those in the group, we didn't finish the course.

In search of answers, I woke up early one morning. The financial freedom class came to mind. Although we had stopped attending, I decided to complete the exercises in my workbook alone. The book was collecting dust, so I mustered up the strength to pull it out of the closet.

While I was seated at the kitchen table, I thoughtfully responded to the questions. Then reality hit me. I had forgotten about my calling. The weight of everyday life had crushed my vision. My dreams had utterly slipped away.

At times, life's burdens made the vision hard to see. Even so, it never completely left my mind. Over the years, I crossed paths with people who spoke other languages. I was rusty at first, but my ability to speak came back almost instantly. With language came vision: a reflection of greater things to come.

In need of guidance, I prayed a simple prayer and then spoke aloud, "God, if you help me with this situation, I promise that I will pursue my calling. I will speak the languages again. I will do my part."

God wasn't delayed in answering my prayer. I found the courage to start the process with our housing situation that Monday. I was scheduled to go to the office in South Florida the following week.

When I arrived at the office, my boss approached me with interesting news. "Julie, the team will call Europe in a month. We know you speak Spanish, Portuguese and Italian. You will be calling Spain, Portugal and Italy." While I was shocked, I wasn't surprised. God was faithful. He gave me the courage to take a step, and I had to hold to my end of the bargain.

Frankly, I hadn't used the languages for years. I was nervous yet up to the challenge. I went to the bookstore that weekend and walked out with a stack of books. From that day forward, I consistently used the languages for work.

At the start of my journey, I knew that I was supposed to learn French as well. I chose not to pursue it, but it was never far from my mind. Many years later, my sales manager approached me with a question. "Julie, are you willing to learn French?" I quickly responded, "No, I don't have the time or the energy to learn another language." The conversation didn't leave my mind that weekend. I came back the following week and agreed to learn.

God had given me much and with that came much responsibility. I knew what I was supposed to do. Like a shadow in the dark, the gift of language gave me the faith to follow through.

Each time I learned a language, I changed. My thinking changed, and I had to recreate myself. I couldn't live in the past. Languages were a part of the vision, and the vision was my future.

God gave me a shadow in the dark so that I wouldn't give up. At times, I tried to push the gift away. While it would have been easier to settle, it was with me to stay.

The real message isn't about words spoken or written. It's about hope. I wasn't left to wonder. I was given no reason to doubt. I was blessed with the gift so that I would never forget.

The real message isn't about words spoken or written. It's about hope. I wasn't left to wonder. I was given no reason to doubt.

Yes, my shadow in the dark was a reflection of what was to come. It also helped me to leave the past in the past. I was in every scene twice for a reason. I needed to accept who I was, and I needed to remember who I was called to be.

With my attention back to the tour, God spoke through images on the wall. "Having then gifts differing according to the grace that is given to us, *let us use them:*" (Romans 12:6 NKJV).

———————

VISION KEEPS THE DREAM ALIVE.
THE LIGHT IS ALWAYS ON. NOTHING CAN PUT IT OUT.

SOMETIMES WE LOSE DIRECTION TO FIND OUR WAY.
GRACE BRINGS US BACK, STRONGER THAN BEFORE.

———————

Julie Barbera

9 | Unbroken Dreams

"For we are God's handiwork,
created in Christ Jesus to do good works,
which God prepared in advance for us to do."

(Ephesians 2:10 NIV)

W ould I leave a legacy or live with broken dreams? Either
way, I was created with a purpose. The vision was clear.
Although courage was hard to find, I wasn't willing to give up on
my dream. I would always wonder what might have happened
had I taken a chance.

Vision gave life meaning. My pursuit was to find purpose. I
tended to chase goals, and most had nothing to do with my call-

ing. Chasing goals led to forgetting dreams. Aiming for the target, I completely missed the mark.

As usual, I woke up early to write. My family and I had just returned from Saint Augustine. The trip inspired me, yet I returned more confused than ever. At a loss for words, I pondered why it had taken so many years to do the obvious. I knew what I was called to do. While it seemed logical to step into it with confidence, I couldn't even take the smallest of steps.

Writing seemed to help, even if I never reread what I wrote. The mere act of jotting down thoughts brought the truth to light. I scribbled on a piece of paper, crumbled it up and then set it to the side. Frankly, I was accustomed to putting things aside.

Every child has a fantasy, and every man and woman has a dream. Dreams grow out of imagination, and imagination is where the heart lives. All things are possible. While the vision made sense in my mind, I lacked understanding in my heart.

Dreams grow out of imagination, and imagination is where the heart lives. All things are possible.

At times, I was in touch with what I felt to be my purpose. A majority of the time, life seemed to lack meaning. Daily life made me feel ordinary. Sadly, I didn't feel worthy of dreams.

Although goals kept me going, empty goals would never fill the void. Emptiness always prompted me to chase, yet again, another goal. In search of purpose, I sought something to make me feel complete.

It seemed I was chasing after the wind. In reality, I was avoiding the obvious. It took courage to pursue goals, even useless ones. *Why was I unable to step into what I knew to be my calling?*

The vision was blurred. I lacked direction, yet my purpose

was clear. I was certain clarity would come in time. Maybe, just maybe, the perfect moment hadn't yet arrived.

Life took me down some dark, empty roads. Even so, there was always a reason. Valuable lessons were learned along the way, and every lesson had its share of blessings.

Over time I drifted far from the vision. The further I drifted, the harder it was to envision my dreams becoming a reality. Even so, they never completely left my mind.

Suddenly, the vision returned. My family and I were back in Saint Augustine. Time subtly stood still. I watched as we strolled down historic streets paved with memories.

The journey led us to a museum. As spectators, we enjoyed the legacy that others had left behind. Every work of art was another's dream. Beauty before our eyes was someone's destiny. Dreams lived on and on through the contributions made.

Art is created to inspire. Literature is written to prompt thought, and music is produced to bring out feelings. Others' accomplishments were supposed to encourage me. Regretfully, what I felt was the opposite.

Envy, jealousy and regret, these were ugly feelings. I didn't like them, but I couldn't deny them. While such sentiments weren't conducive to success, I still felt what I felt. I wanted to be happy for others. I wanted to feel inspired, and I wanted that inspiration to drive my success. Instead, I felt stuck.

Contemplating the mark of another, a thought arose, *What legacy will I leave behind?* Every moment is a gift, and every day is a treasure. I wanted to seize the moment. *But, how?*

Seemingly, much time had been wasted. Yet, I couldn't take a pen and erase the past. Wishing life had been lived differently wouldn't change the present. The past was the past. While it wasn't possible to make up for the lost time, I needed to make the most of today.

Inspired, I scribbled a few words in my notepad. Don't dwell on how you wish things were, how you think they should be. Make the best of what they are.

I had spent years waiting for the perfect moment. The past was gone. The future somehow felt within reach, but the present was all I had. A thought came to mind. *Progress isn't just what you do to move forward. It's what you leave behind to keep moving.*

Contemplating the mark of another, a thought arose, *What legacy will I leave behind?*

Back from Saint Augustine for close to two weeks, memories were fresh in mind. I wasn't much for spontaneity. In fact, I was far more prone to a strict routine. The trip somehow motivated me to break free from the mold.

In search of a way to pass the time, my family and I drove to Fort Lauderdale. We unintentionally ended up in the middle of an art festival. I loved creativity, but I was never one for art or music festivals. I initially didn't want to stay, but I quickly gave in for the kids.

As I strolled downtown, I saw tents lining a crowded street. Everything about the afternoon was perfect. Even so, I noticed a shift in mindset. Negative feelings quickly surfaced. The event sparked a desire within yet touched a sensitive cord.

Approaching a corner tent, I walked close enough to see. A man stood nearby. Anxiously waiting, his eyes were full of hope. Perhaps he had spent months, if not years, in preparation.

The stone sculptures that he had created were to be admired. Every piece was unique. Each one was perfectly shaped and thoughtfully designed. I paused for just a moment and then quickly proceeded to the next tent.

Taking a few steps forward, beautiful paintings caught my attention. A woman was smiling as she proudly stood beside what looked to be her greatest masterpiece. I wondered how many hours had been invested.

Attracted to the beauty and drawn in by detail, I stopped to appreciate her work. The crowd was closing in, so I was forced to move on. I paused briefly and then continued my stroll down the busy street.

Suddenly, bright photographs drew my attention. Picturesque landscapes and settings came to life. Every image captured a moment in time. The beauty of nature made every picture perfect.

God's artwork was to be admired. Still, many hours must have been invested. I wondered what it took to capture such beautiful images. Passersby crowded around the tent. I wanted to stay, but I had to move on to make room for others.

Playing with passion, a talented musician proudly shared his latest album. All appeared soothed as they passed his stand. I paused long enough to listen to a relaxing song. Since there was so much to see and so little time to see it, I had to move on.

On the outside, I looked interested. On the inside, a change took place. Although I appreciated art, I wasn't focused on sculptures, paintings or music. I sought to understand dreams.

As a practical thinker, I needed to make sense of something to do it. It needed to be realistic for me to attempt it. Interestingly, my dream was anything but practical. *One day I would speak in front of thousands in different languages. God would do things to amaze me. How was I supposed to make that practical?*

An ability to learn and speak other languages was clear, tangible evidence. Yet, doubt continuously crept in to dim the vision. Bright future ahead, this was my shadow in the dark. God didn't leave me to wonder. He gave me no reason to doubt, but I was still too blind to see.

Since it was time to tear down, I watched as artists closed up shop. Paintings were carefully taken down. Sculptures were wrapped with care. All wanted to protect treasured works of art.

I pondered the time invested in preparation, set-up and take-down. Some had a successful day, while others would leave empty-handed. I was sure that all had started the day with an expectation of success.

With varying talents and styles, no two artists were alike. Each one wanted to be recognized for unique gifts, yet a common thread united all. Every single artist lining that busy street had a dream.

My dream was my dream, and not everyone would under-stand it. Life was about risk. The possibility of failure was there. Like every artist at the festival, I had to be willing to take a chance.

Suddenly, inspiring words came to mind. *The perfect moment will never arrive. Sometimes you need to take a chance, risk it all for a chance to fly.*

At times, investments would be made with the expectation that others would show appreciation. It wasn't realistic to expect recognition nor could I rely on reactions from others. As a passerby, I didn't share what I was thinking. I didn't say anything positive to encourage the artists, yet they inspired me to look at myself.

Like me, others would travel in and out of my life. If I stepped out, I might not get the recognition deserved. Perhaps I wouldn't see the impact made on others' lives. Maybe those touched wouldn't opt to share their thoughts.

Expectations aside, it was time to step outside my comfort zone. I had to be willing to invest the time, take a chance and accept the possibility of failure. *Was I ready to do this?*

Every artist lining that busy street started the day with an expectation of success. Days, if not months or years, were invested in preparation. The risk was there, but they didn't allow fear to hold them back.

As I stepped away from the crowd, I thought about dreams. This wasn't my first art festival nor would it be my last. While my vision was the same, something changed in my heart that day. I didn't leave with a plan. I walked away with hope.

I didn't discover hidden talents or gain clarity regarding the next step. I left with a changed heart. And for the first time, I was able to appreciate others' accomplishments. An acknowledgment of others' gifts and talents made it possible to focus on what made me unique. In turn, I found the courage to take a chance.

I stopped for a moment and then looked back at the street lined with dreams. Gazing at an empty byway, courage built up inside. Inspired, I carried just enough hope for the journey and left the rest behind.

That day turned into just a memory. But I walked away with hope. Hope gave me the courage to believe that my one day would turn into more than just a dream. Encouraging words reminded me of the truth. "And we know that in all things God works for the good of those who love him, who have been called according to his purpose" (Romans 8:28 NIV).

———

WHAT YOU THINK ABOUT YOURSELF BECOMES YOUR REALITY.
BELIEVE THAT YOU CAN AND YOU WILL.

IF YOU ARE READY TO STEP INTO YOUR POTENTIAL,
BE PREPARED TO STEP OUTSIDE YOUR COMFORT ZONE.

———

Julie Barbera

10 | Beyond the Mirror

"For with God nothing will be impossible."

(Luke 1:37 NKJV)

Would I give in to self-limiting thoughts or find a way to look beyond the mirror? Either way, I resolved to reach my potential. Possibilities were endless, yet I was my most significant limitation. What I achieved would only go as high as what I believed.

Life is the story. God is the author. Vision gave life to dreams. Although my manuscript was incomplete, my account was written in time.

As was my daily routine, I woke up early. I sat at the dining room table with a cup of coffee in hand. Still dark outside, I looked out the window. Instantly, I was back at the art festival.

Dreams somehow made more sense that morning. Confident in my purpose, I still struggled with doubt. While the vision didn't change, how I viewed it had changed.

My dream was my dream, and not everyone would understand it. If I stepped out, there would be some risk. Trying meant I might fail. Still, my vision would never be more than just a thought without the courage to take a chance.

Life is the story. God is the author. Vision gave life to dreams. Although my manuscript was incomplete, my account was written in time.

I had a mental image of artists lined up in small tents along a crowded street. They had diverse talents and styles, and no two creators were the same. All came with a purpose. Each one waited for recognition, and a common thread united all of them. Every single artist lining that busy street had a dream.

As I stepped away from the crowd, I thought about my vision. I arrived full of envy and regret. I didn't leave with a plan, but I walked away with hope.

I stopped for a moment and then looked back at the street lined with dreams. As I gazed at an empty byway, courage built up inside. Inspired, I carried just enough confidence for the journey and left the rest behind.

Suddenly, my family and I were in the car. Driving home that evening, I looked up at a beautiful sunset as day turned to night. The art festival prompted all of us to examine dreams more closely.

The conversation quickly shifted to college for our two young sons. They had big plans for the future. They were full of potential, and the possibilities were endless. The world was at their fingertips. Both believed they could become anything they wanted to be.

As a parent, I wanted to give them the world. My dream was for them to prosper. At just seven and ten years old, my boys were full of faith. In many ways, they were wise beyond their years.

While I was happy about the bright future ahead, I was also saddened. In the not so distant future, my sons would be out in the world all grown up. I had a vision of them making a difference, living the life of their dreams and fulfilling their God-given purpose.

Days like this wouldn't last forever. If only I could bottle the moment. Time spent with my children made me realize how fast time had passed. One day I was rocking them to sleep, feeding them a bottle and changing pampers. Then, they were all grown up. I wished they could stay young forever.

My mind wandered back in time as the sun began its descent below the horizon. With my full life ahead, I was trying to figure out the world. It felt like yesterday. I was similar to my sons in many ways, yet I was very different in others. I had dreams, but not the kind they shared with me. I didn't dream of becoming a doctor, sports star or famous artist, at least not at their age.

While I watched my younger self intently, I saw my hands over my ears and a pillow over my face. Alone in my room at ten years old, I cried myself to sleep. While I desired peace above all else, I lacked the courage to dream big. Deep inside, I felt unworthy of dreams.

Almost home, I was present in time. My children were still considering all of the possibilities ahead. Then I realized, I was living my childhood dream. Taking special moments like these for granted was no longer an option. Wasting another day just getting through the day was out of the question. Not pursuing dreams held in my heart was no longer a choice.

Reflections from the past, present and future were visible.

Self-limiting thoughts crept in from time to time. Although my mirror had its fair share of cracks, I resolved to look beyond them. Insecurities that once stopped me had lost the power to control me.

The vision didn't change. Even so, my perception had changed. Up to this point, I saw life through half-empty glasses. Beyond the mirror, challenges and limitations seemed smaller. Half-full glasses made potential and possibilities appear so much taller.

Although my mirror had its fair share of cracks, I resolved to look beyond them. Insecurities that once stopped me had lost the power to control me.

With my eyes fixed on the nighttime sky, a few stars were shining brightly. The vision was more apparent than ever. My children and I suddenly stood out among the stars. When I was prompted to look down at my phone, a message came through.

"But one thing I do: Forgetting what is behind and straining toward what is ahead, I press on toward the goal to win the prize for which God has called me heavenward in Christ Jesus" (Philippians 3:13-14 NIV).

SOME FEEL THAT IMPERFECTIONS
MAKE THEM UNWORTHY OF GOD'S PLAN.
THIS IS FAR FROM THE TRUTH.
IT'S THESE FLAWS THAT WILL BE USED FOR HIS GLORY.

Julie Barbera

11 | Changed in Season

"To everything *there is* a season,
A time for every purpose under heaven:"

(Ecclesiastes 3:1 NKJV)

Would seasons change or would I be changed in season? Either way, everything happened for a reason. Grace followed the cold of winter. Spring brought hope, and summer welcomed freedom. A feeling of renewal came with the freshness of fall. Perhaps a meaningful story would be found in all.

My journey began with a paintbrush, pen and pencil. A story was written in time. My voice was my paintbrush. It was used to paint a portrait of my life. With my canvas set aside for a season, I picked up my pen to write.

It was early morning, and I sat at the dining room table. Pen in hand, I reflected on stages of life. The inspiration came unexpectedly. Childhood memories crossed paths with the present moment. A trip to a botanical garden brought the truth to light.

Suddenly back in the garden with my husband and two young sons, a valuable story began to unfold. Trees don't speak, yet their presence whispered through the cold. Oak trees stood tall. They towered over all. I wondered how many seasons they had seen, how many stories had been left untold.

As a child, I stood beside a frosted window. A blanket of white covered grass and trees. Branches were weighed down, and trees stood bare. Street lights reflected off the snow. Lying on my back, I formed snow angels. Gazing up at a nighttime sky, I flew high among the stars.

Years later, I stood beside the same window. When I was finally old enough to leave, I discreetly snuck out the front door. Running through a wintry storm, a mist formed with every breath. I made it to the high school running track. Alone in the dark, I ran against the wind.

These were cherished days of winter. Many lasted longer than desired. Others were best left unremembered. Some warmed the heart, yet all were frozen in time. A snowman stood in front of Grandma's house. It would soon melt under the warmth of the sun.

Grace followed the cold of winter. Hope came with the arrival of spring. Longing to enjoy freedom, I gazed out the window and then quickly made my way to the front door. The lightness of spring was in my midst.

Blue jays and cardinals were perched on a small birdhouse. Pink and red roses blossomed all around. A family of mallards greeted me in the yard. Seated high on a large branch, I looked down at tomatoes and strawberries below. The heat of the sun was blocked by large branches. Protected by large, green leaves, I felt safe.

During the spring of childhood, many treasured memories were locked away in my heart for a lifetime. Hopscotch in the street and long walks with friends, these were days to be remembered. This season of simplicity always flew by quicker than desired. I wished carefree days like these would last forever. Hope came at just the right time, and any trace of worry dissipated under the warmth of the sun.

With cameras in hand, my children and I wanted to capture the moment. As we enjoyed the day while strolling through tranquil gardens, God spoke through a calm spring breeze. "He made the moon to mark the seasons, and the sun knows when to go down" (Psalm 104:19 NIV). Admiring beauty all around, I pondered the seasons.

All pass through times of struggle. Through even the stormiest of days, we must learn to dance in the rain.

All pass through times of struggle. Through even the stormiest of days, we must learn to dance in the rain. Every tree, butterfly and small blade of grass goes through seasons. God sets everything in motion, and all is in His hands.

Many pass through seasons of life without acknowledging their beauty. It's possible to arrive at an old age never to have appreciated the rising and the setting of the sun. It's conceivable to have walked through life never to have noticed the miracle of flowers in bloom or a fresh spring breeze.

When we were approaching a lake surrounded by flowers and trees, my family and I noticed four bright orange butterflies. Playing together, they gracefully danced around a garden. Wanting to capture just one photo, we waited patiently with cameras in hand. All four butterflies appeared for a moment and then fluttered away.

Gazing at butterflies frolicking around, a thought came to mind. *We chase life like we chase butterflies to snap a picture. We blink, and the butterfly is gone. Capture the moment today.*

Many of us arrive at a season of life only to await the coming of the next. Winter comes, and we anticipate spring. Spring arrives, and we can't wait for summer. The heat of summer makes us long for fall.

As young adults, we long to go to college to experience freedom. Once in college, we can't wait to graduate to get out into the real world. After graduation, the pursuit is a successful life. There is always another target to reach. At times, chasing goals leads to forgetting dreams. Aiming for the target, we completely miss the mark.

We frequently stopped to take family photos. No trace of this glorious spring day would be forgotten. My sons were in their springtime in full bloom. God had graciously given me another chance to make the most of the life I had been given.

Grateful to finally see and no longer chasing after the wind, I had arrived at a season of thankfulness. Having passed through many seasons, I realized how quickly time had gone by. Like a butterfly in flight or a flower in due season, I was ready to appreciate each and every day.

Cobblestones were on the ground, and vine plants spiraled all around me. I pondered the road all walk in life as I admired a well-formed passageway. At every crossroads, choices are there to be made. The destination is determined by paths chosen along the way.

Since I realized that springtime wouldn't last forever, I reflected on summer. It would arrive in the coming months. Flowers would soak in rays from the sun. Like a blazing torch, heat would cover the earth.

It was the season of sowing; all was in preparation for an autumn harvest. I sipped ice cold lemonade, enjoyed a refreshing watermelon and went for a rejuvenating swim in the pool.

Although this was my time to play, I still couldn't wait to escape the heat.

I was awakened by the sound of roosters crowing, and the sun lit up my room. I got up quickly to look out the window. Soothed by the sound of birds singing, I felt a feeling of freedom in the air. I was free, free at last. Summer vacation was here.

My friends and I walked to the ice cream parlor. We ran freely in an open field in search of four-leaf clovers. These were days to be remembered. While time seemed to stand still under the warmth of the sun, I couldn't wait for fall to arrive.

Summertime as a child makes many long for freedom. Others can't wait to escape the heat. Since they are never satisfied, they long for another season. Time is spent wishing days away.

Flowers and leaves had passed through budding of spring and blossoming of summer. They would soon dry up. Leaves would change color, wither and fall. Some would survive the cold of winter, while others would have to wait for spring.

Continuing my stroll, I was surrounded by delightful bonsai trees. Every one of these miniature trees told a story. Each represented a season. All took me back in time. One, in particular, caught my attention. Yellow, red and green leaves covered a tiny oak tree. Autumn was always a preferred season of mine.

At times, I would change in season. Other times, I struggled with transition more than I would like to admit. Every stage of life had a purpose. Through it all, I found the courage to write my story.

Colored leaves piled in the yard made for the perfect place to jump. Landing on my back, I gazed up at beautiful oak trees standing high under a vast, blue sky. Renewal of fall gave me another chance to try.

Seasons would undoubtedly change, and growth was inevitable. At times, I would change in season. Other times, I struggled with transition more than I would like to admit. Every stage of life had a purpose. Through it all, I found the courage to write my story.

God's grace was present in every season, even during the coldest of winters. Spring rain was a reminder that winter had come to an end. I was more determined than ever to press through winter storms, endure summer heat and push through the dryness of fall.

Crossing a quaint bridge, I was greeted by beautifully shaped bonsai trees. Nothing is perfect of course, yet all happens in God's perfect timing. I turned around midway and was able to see all the way across the lake. Words of inspiration reflected off the water as I took my last shot. "For I know the plans I have for you," declares the Lord, "plans to prosper you and not to harm you, plans to give you hope and a future" (Jeremiah 29:11 NIV).

WE CHASE LIFE LIKE WE CHASE BUTTERFLIES TO SNAP A PICTURE.
WE BLINK, AND THE BUTTERFLY IS GONE.
CAPTURE THE MOMENT TODAY.

Julie Barbera

12 | A New Reflection

"Forget the former things; do not dwell on the past.
See, I am doing a new thing!
Now it springs up; do you not perceive it?"

(Isaiah 43:18-19 NIV)

W ould I step into the future with confidence or let doubt
hold me back? Either way, a change was inevitable. The
vision was clear. While I dreamed of what was to come, it was a
challenge to move forward while looking back. Perhaps if I let go
of the old, I would find the courage to embrace the new.

Life took me down both rocky and straight paths. Every path
led to valuable lessons. Some were enjoyable, while others were

less than desirable. All had a purpose. Even the most difficult of days ended with a chance to start again.

For years, I visualized a brighter future. Even so, worry crushed the vision. In deep thought about new beginnings, it was one of those days when dreams felt impossible. Seemingly limited by circumstances, I lacked courage.

When I visited the park with family, small seeds covered the sidewalk. Many were crushed. Others were vulnerable yet still intact. Scattered among flower buds, even the tiniest seed had a second chance.

That day ended as many come and then drift away with the wind. Perhaps I would get a glimpse of better days ahead. Maybe, just maybe, I would gain insight into what it really means to start again.

As I did most days, I woke up early. Notebook ready with a pen in hand, mornings were my time to reflect. I needed the inspiration to write. I never imagined it would come from something as small as a seed.

Suddenly back in the park, the message was clear. Scattered seeds, just like broken dreams, left the door open for grace. Blown by the wind, the destination was uncertain. Yet, the real purpose was found in brokenness.

For years, I had supposedly lost my way. Even so, I wasn't lost. My path felt uncertain, yet my vision for the future was clear. I thought to myself, *Sometimes we lose direction to find our way. Grace brings us back, stronger than before.*

Complicating the simple had distorted the truth. I had gone through seasons in life, just as nature has its seasons. At times, leaves went from brown to green as

Sometimes we lose direction to find our way. Grace brings us back, stronger than before.

flowers bloomed. Other times, leaves went from green to brown as flowers wilted and fell. And every season had a purpose.

Surrounded by cheerful colors, flowers were in full bloom. A feeling of newness was in the air. As much as I enjoyed the serenity of the day, the storms of winter had prepared me for the comfort of spring.

While I reflected on new beginnings, the message was clear. All along I had been searching for a destination, but I would never find it in a season or a day. God's grace gave me unending chances. I didn't lack direction. What I needed was to trust. Then, I would find my way.

Progress isn't just what you do to move forward. It's what you leave behind to keep moving. Although I was inspired, the idea of a new thing was overwhelming. I wanted to step into the future with confidence, yet I clung to the familiarity of the past.

Progress isn't just what you do to move forward. It's what you leave behind to keep moving.

The setting quickly changed. A hidden path led to a wooded area. In the distance, beautiful butterflies fluttered around a bed of wildflowers. Curious, I followed the trail.

Since I was captivated by the scene, I couldn't just pass by with disregard. Although busyness made it hard to stop, it was a challenge to move forward. Something about that moment forced me to look at life differently. I paused long enough to enjoy the view.

A thought came to mind. *At times, we are chasing life just like we chase butterflies to snap a picture. We blink, and the butterfly is gone.* I needed to capture the moment. But how?

Suddenly, a caterpillar emerged. It was hard to imagine that it would soon turn into a graceful butterfly. The small creature crawled by and then devoured a tiny leaf and egg. Other cater-pillars rested on neighboring leaves. Each varied in size and color. All were at different stages of growth.

Once again, my attention shifted to butterflies dancing in the distance. With a camera in hand, I walked close enough to snap a picture. Although it was hard to get a clear shot, I captured the moment in my mind.

Every butterfly had gone through the process of metamor-phosis. While painful, it happened naturally. I had a tendency to resist change. Resistance halted forward progress. I needed to let go and embrace change with grace.

Drawn to a lake adjacent to a wooded area, moths fluttered around. While they lacked the beauty of butterflies, they still had a purpose. The final product was different, yet the process of transformation was the same. A dull brown color made them less attractive. In fact, they were downright unattractive. Regardless of appearance, all was by God's unique design.

Perhaps I thought I was looking at a butterfly when in reality I was gazing at a moth. Or, maybe I perceived a butterfly as dull and unattractive because I thought it was a moth. Either way, I had judged by outer appearance.

Every creature is born with a purpose, and value isn't measured by perception. Butterflies and moths are a part of a more excellent plan. I wasn't an expert on either. *So, why was I so quick to judge?*

Suddenly, the reflection was clear. Through my cracked mirror, I measured value by external appearance. Many times, I was far too quick to judge myself and others. In fact, I didn't even allow the truth to be revealed because I had already made up my mind.

As I walked away from the lake, I acknowledged a need to accept myself and others at every stage of growth. Some would be painful and ugly. Others would be effortless and beautiful. Whatever the case, every phase would have significance.

Although a new reflection made it possible to move forward, I still struggled with my share of doubt. I learned to accept insecurity and uncertainty as a part of the process. I did look back at times but only long enough to reflect. Rather than resist change, I allowed it to change me. Judgment and bias behind, I stepped into the new thing.

With my family by my side, I made my way to the parking lot. The park was ready to close, and we were there much longer than expected. I was usually in a rush. That day I chose to slow down.

All of a sudden, the conversation shifted to butterflies. Amazed at a picture of a beautiful butterfly, I looked closer. I didn't say anything, but it was actually a moth. My kids always caught the moments that I missed. This time I captured the moment in my mind.

When we were ready to back up, I rolled my window down for just a second. A butterfly fluttered by and then landed on the fence in front of our car. I jumped out to take one last shot. I didn't have to chase the butterfly this time. It just was, and I caught it on camera.

With my phone in hand, I looked down to check out an email. Inspiration always came through at just the right time. "See, the former things have taken place, and new things I declare; before they spring into being I announce them to you" (Isaiah 42:9 NIV).

A DESIRE TO CHANGE NEEDS TO BE
STRONGER THAN FEAR OF CHANGE.
THEN YOU'LL FIND THE COURAGE TO TAKE A STEP.

Julie Barbera

13 | Perfect Imperfection

"And we all, who with unveiled faces contemplate the
Lord's glory, are being transformed into his image
with ever-increasing glory, which comes from the
Lord, who is the spirit."

(2 Corinthians 3:18 NIV)

Would I recreate how life should be or use what I have to create a better experience? Either way, life went on. Perfection was the standard, and I wondered who had set the bar. It was clear my vision wasn't going to change. Perhaps I needed to change my view of reality.

Life wasn't perfect, and it never would be. Still, I was more concerned with righting wrongs than doing what I knew to be right. My vision for the future was clear. But clarity didn't equate to perfection. The truth be known, there was a crack in my perception.

Through my cracked mirror, I measured truth by what was seen. Circumstances weren't ideal. Yet, I gave them far more power than deserved. I wanted to move forward, but I chose to wait rather than risk being wrong.

As usual, my morning started early. Pen in hand, I was at a loss for words. Memories crossed paths with the present moment. As I reflected on the past, I found the inspiration to create a new story. Since I was ready to write the next chapter, it was time to turn the page.

Through my cracked mirror, I measured truth by what was seen. Circumstances weren't ideal. Yet, I gave them far more power than deserved.

Happily ever after was how I saw life as a child. As an adult, my happy still waited for *ever after.* One day felt closer than ever, yet it seemed it would never arrive. If for just an instant, my one day came to life.

My family and I were at the mall. While wandering around just passing the time, my youngest son spotted toys in the distance. Without hesitation, he darted into a store. Following close behind, I ended up halfway between dolls and cars.

In the toy store, I saw life through the eyes of a child. Since I was all grown up, my view of the world had changed. Childhood ideals seemed far behind. And the truth would only be revealed through a trip back in time.

One side of the store was clearly marked for boys, the other for girls. Cars, airplanes and superheroes captured my son's attention. I was attracted to castles, princesses and dolls. I gazed across the room and went back to a season of innocence.

Every boy and girl dreams of being all grown up. The expectation is that once upon a time will end in happily ever after. While I had my eyes fixed on princess dolls, I saw a vision of my dreams as a child. In every fairy tale, there was a happy ending. A damsel in distress going through difficult times was rescued by a knight in shining armor. Good overcame evil. All would live happily ever after.

My mind drifted back to the moment, and I watched intently as my younger son played with toy cars and airplanes. Attracted to a sword and shield, he ran across the room. Present in the moment, his imagination was in full gear. Since I was unable to understand a young boy's mind, I had no idea what he was thinking. Maybe he imagined himself as a knight in shining armor rescuing a damsel in distress. Perhaps he visualized himself conquering evil, all with the hope of good prevailing and living happily ever after.

My son wanted to take all of the toys home. When it was almost time to go, he refused to leave without them. He held on tight to newfound treasures and then made his escape to the opposite side of the store.

Looking around, I noticed other parents going through the same thing. Across the room, I spotted a little girl dressed in a princess dress, crown and shoes. The mother, anxious to leave, told her that it was time to go. The little girl quickly threw herself on the floor and screamed, "I want to be a princess, Mommy. I want to be a princess."

Having young children, somewhat accustomed to this behavior, I wasn't shocked. The mindset of a child seems to be hardwired to *I want what I want when I want it. I want it now.*

Drawn into the scene, I noticed a fancy, pink and purple toy castle on the floor. The little girl went into the castle, curled up in a ball and refused to come out. My son ran over to a red sports car on the opposite side of the store. Once inside, he didn't want to leave.

Watching the scene unfold, I began to reflect. This behavior, while very typical for young children, strongly resembles the mindset of some adults. Daydreaming for just a moment, I imagined my son and the little girl all grown up.

Focused on being a princess, the young woman spends much of her time on primping. Hair, nails, makeup, outfit and shoes, everything needs to be perfect. She longs to meet Mr. Right: her knight in shining armor.

She is disappointed to find that no man measures up to her expectations. None even come close to her childhood dream. Still, she hopes to find a fairy tale love that will sweep her off her feet.

The young man searches for his princess. Once found, he wants to give her the world. Working day and night, his goal is to save enough to buy a bigger castle and a fancier carriage.

The knight in shining armor meets the princess. They have a vision of riding off into the night. Both hold on to a dream of living happily ever after. While the focus is on fulfilling childhood fantasies, life doesn't go as planned.

The knight will never be as charming as imagined. The princess will never look perfect all the time. Unable to cope with a disconnect between dreams and reality, they quickly give up.

The princess is no longer happy with her castle and carriage. She wants to impress and won't settle for less. The prince loses interest in her outer beauty and looks for another princess.

The princess meets another knight, but he still doesn't measure up. The knight meets another princess, but he quickly realizes that she isn't as perfect as he thought. Wondering what happened to happily ever after, both are left frustrated and confused.

As I drifted back from a daydream, I realized I had held on to childhood fantasies for years. Since I recognized how much this had limited me, I was ready to let go of the old and make the best of my reality.

Every good story comes to an end. That day turned into nothing more than just a memory. Yet, I had my chance to dream. Halfway between what was and what could be, I wondered if my one day would come again.

While I dreamed of how life should be, I spent far too many days trying to match my vision with reality.

While I dreamed of how life should be, I spent far too many days trying to match my vision with reality. A clear picture was in my mind about the perfect marriage, model family, successful career and ideal life. Once I was able to make the best of my reality, I would find my happy ending.

In pursuit of perfection, I tried to have more, do more and be more. Honestly, there was nothing wrong with wanting to be better. But there was something wrong with nothing being good enough.

My one day was somehow tied to a life that wasn't my own. Expectations for the future came from somewhere unknown. The truth revealed, my life was something that I needed to own. It wasn't perfect, and it never would be.

Since it was time to turn the page, I was ready to accept the life I had been given. It was through acceptance that I would create a better experience. With perfect imperfection, I would use my gifts and talents. I not only needed to use them, but I also needed to be bold enough to step outside of my comfort zone. Above all else, I needed to accept that things wouldn't always turn out perfectly.

As I walked out of the store, I caught a glimpse of my image. Words of wisdom reflected off the window. "When I was a child,

I talked like a child, I thought like a child, I reasoned like a child. When I became a man, I put the ways of childhood behind me. For now we see only a reflection as in a mirror; then we shall see face to face. Now I know in part; then I shall know fully, even as I am fully known" (1 Corinthians 13:11-12 NIV).

———

**DON'T DWELL ON HOW YOU WISH THINGS WERE,
HOW YOU THINK THEY SHOULD BE.
MAKE THE BEST OF WHAT THEY ARE.**

**IF YOU CAN'T CHANGE CIRCUMSTANCES,
CHANGE THE WAY YOU LOOK AT THEM. LOOK FOR THE POSITIVE.**

———

Julie Barbera

14 | On Eagle's Wings

"He shielded him and cared for him;
he guarded him as the apple of his eye,
like an eagle that stirs up its nest and
hovers over its young, that spreads its
wings to catch them and carries them aloft."

(Deuteronomy 32:10-11 NIV)

Would I skim the surface or take off in flight? Either way, I felt ready. Awaiting the perfect moment, it seemed it would never arrive. Going deep was painful. Reaching high was risky. Neither guaranteed success. Perhaps I just needed the courage to take a chance.

A desire to excel was admirable, but want without action

wouldn't take me far. I soared just above the water. Close enough to skim the surface, it felt safe to touch the edge.

While my manuscript was more than just an idea, it wasn't quite a book. I wrote day after day, and this simple act made the vision come to life. Even so, I wasn't quite ready to move from words to action.

Today started like most days. Since I was determined to make it count, I woke up early. A daily routine kept me on track. If nothing else, I saw progress on paper. Still, I wanted more. Frustrated yet inspired, I began to write.

Motion unrestricted, I mounted up with wings like an eagle. With my arms spread wide, I flew high. Free, free alas, I soared through a clear, blue sky. Those on the ground gazed up in amazement as I reached heights never imagined possible.

While I was in control of my destiny, nothing felt impossible. The world somehow looked different from above. Everything looked smaller, and problems seemed to dissipate.

For years, I wanted to be free. While this was just a dream, the feeling of freedom was real. This wasn't my first time experiencing such a vision nor would it be my last. A dreamer at heart, I believed I would one day get my chance. Disappointed that my wings were clipped, I wondered if this was just a sign. Though I lacked the courage to step out, the vision never entirely left my mind.

A desire to excel was admirable, but want without action wouldn't take me far. I soared just above the water. Close enough to skim the surface, it felt safe to touch the edge.

The following day, I was at the park with my family. Drawn to birds in flight, I thought about my dream the night prior. I wanted freedom, yet I held on to control. If I genuinely wanted to be free, I needed to let go.

Watching my children play in the distance, my husband and I stayed back in the shadows. They needed space. We gave them the room to explore. Walking side by side, they were learning about the world. They longed for independence. At the same time, they had developed an increased dependence on one another.

Ready to spread their wings, my little boys were growing up. Since they trusted that we were waiting in the wings, they walked forward with confidence. They were out of our sight for just a few minutes, and I began to get nervous. Suddenly, they emerged from a hidden trail.

Proudly carrying sticks, they ran toward us with confidence. Though simplistic, these sticks represented something significant. They were a symbol of freedom and trust. We gave them freedom. They trusted that we were there watching over them.

Since my sons wanted to play, I stopped to rest on a nearby bench. As I listened to the birds sing, all began to make sense. Birds are under the shadow of God's wings, and they spread far and wide. Just as He cares and provides for them, He cares and provides for us. Children are under the shadow of our wings. Acknowledging God's protection gives us the confidence to let go and trust.

At home that evening, I was alone in my room. Surrounded by the sounds of the night, I pondered the idea of being totally free. Crickets chirped outside my window as I drifted into a light sleep.

Close to the edge, I saw my reflection. Able to touch the water, I felt secure. I wanted to let go, yet freedom didn't equate to protection. Sadly, I never made it off the ground. Merely coasting, I wondered, *Where did white, fluffy clouds go? What happened to the beautiful skyline?*

Ready to step out, I longed to mount up with wings like an

eagle. Even so, something weighed me down. When I was off the ground yet skimming the surface, something held me back.

In the distance, I spotted a bird with its wings spread wide. Standing on a rock, it waited for them to dry. Then another bird dove into the lake. It didn't swim or go too deep. It merely bobbed in place with its head above the water.

Suddenly, the bird emerged from the water and stood along the edge. Since its wings were wet, it was unable to fly. Soaking in rays, both birds stood beside the lake. Neither swimming nor flying, they waited for the perfect moment to take off in flight.

Close to the water's edge, I saw my reflection. Like these birds, I lacked the courage to go too deep or soar too high. It felt safe to skim the surface, and my wings were never quite dry enough to mount up. Awaiting the perfect moment, I never took off.

For years, I felt like an eaglet trapped in a nest flapping its wings. At times, I made it off the ground. Much of the time, I waited for someone to come along and rescue me. In all honesty, I lacked the courage to take a chance.

Since I wanted to leave the nest, I dreamed of spreading my wings. A few times I tried but without success. Trees were within reach. I knew I could make it. Yet, the thought always arose, *What if I try and fail?*

Surrounded by walls made of sticks and brush, I stayed within the safety of the familiar. Anticipating being carried away by mighty wings, I dreamed of being rescued from uncertainty. Envisioning myself soaring from tree to

Envisioning myself soaring from tree to tree and branch to branch, I watched in awe as other eaglets risked it all for a chance to fly.

tree and branch to branch, I watched in awe as other eaglets risked it all for a chance to fly.

Although I took off at times, I went just high enough to feel good about my progress. But I stayed close enough to turn back. Going too deep or reaching too high involved risk. Neither came with a guarantee of success.

At a turning point, I realized the perfect moment would never arrive. Since I was no longer trapped in an illusion, God was calling me to go higher. As I walked home with my head held high, I was ready to mount up with wings like an eagle. More in tune with birds in flight, I looked up. Words of hope were written in the sky.

"He gives strength to the weary and increases the power of the weak. Even youths grow tired and weary, and young men stumble and fall; but those who hope in the Lord will renew their strength. They will soar on wings like eagles; they will run and not grow weary, they will walk and not be faint" (Isaiah 40:29-31 NIV).

**THE PERFECT MOMENT WILL NEVER ARRIVE.
SOMETIMES YOU NEED TO TAKE A CHANCE,
RISK IT ALL FOR A CHANCE TO FLY.**

Julie Barbera

15 | Run the Race

"Do you not know that in a race all the runners run,
but only one gets the prize? Run in such a way as
to get the prize."

(1 Corinthians 9:24 NIV)

Would I step on the field or stand along the sidelines? Either way, the game had begun. My position was defense. The goal was to win, and my one move was to block mistakes. Perhaps I needed an offensive strategy to stay in the game.

In many ways, I had already stepped on the field. I woke up every day to write. I bought a domain, and I even built a website. My vision represented independence. Freedom to fulfill my calling was the goal. Even so, my next move was highly dependent on others' reactions.

My family and I went to a soccer game on Saturday evening. Thoughts about the event were still in mind when I awoke Sunday morning. A clear connection was made between soccer and the game of life. With a cup of coffee in hand, I began to write.

Although I resolved to move forward, my next move was uncertain. I was decided in many ways, yet I wondered how I would dance with courage when I still wrestled with doubt.

I was decided in many ways, yet I wondered how I would dance with courage when I still wrestled with doubt.

As I anticipated the event, my energy was at a peak. The crowd cheered as players warmed up on the field. A large screen was positioned above the goal. The countdown to the start of the game had begun, and I watched as time ticked away.

Suddenly, a bird soared over the screen. All alone, it flew high. Almost sunset, yellowish-orange streaks lit up the sky. Bluish-grey clouds peeked through as dusk approached. My eyes were off the scoreboard, and my focus shifted to a glorious show as day turned to night.

Players ran up and down the field. All had one focus in mind: to kick the ball into the goal. Every player had a role, some offense, and others defense. All had to play according to the rules.

Offensive players eagerly chased the ball. Many were in pursuit, but only one had the prized possession. Defense blocked in an attempt to keep opposing players away. With eyes fixed on the prize, the ball was passed to offense. One player was tasked with protecting the goal. Standing in position, he was alert at all times.

Another group waited in the wings. Some would get the opportunity to play, while others would leave without stepping on the field. All of them had trained hard to prepare for the game. Players ran in circles to stay agile. They needed to be ready should their name be called.

Makeshift musical instruments created noise, and the sounds resonated across the field. As dedicated fans shouted with excitement, they pounded the stands. They were dressed in team colors, and their faces were painted to match. Since they were serious fans to the end, they followed the team to every event. Though they were just dedicated bystanders to others, every person in the group felt like an insider.

With five minutes left in the game, the score was zero-zero. The intensity was at a peak as athletes fought harder than ever. Fans and players alike, all wanted to experience the thrill of a win.

Emotion intensified as the clock approached the two-minute mark. Offense stayed close to the goal in an attempt to score. Defense aggressively blocked every shot.

My mind wandered away from the field as I thought about the real game: the race all must run to win the prize. Every player has a position, sometimes offense, and other times defense.

With my focus back to the game with thirty seconds remaining, I contemplated the purpose of a zero-zero finish. Players had pushed through challenges. All had struggled to reach the goal. The objective was to score, yet it appeared that neither team would walk away with a win.

My eyes were fixed on the scoreboard as seconds ticked away. Then, a thought came to mind. *By stepping on the field and staying in the game, half the battle was won.*

The sound of a buzzer echoed across the field, and the game

was officially over. As I walked away, I listened as fans expressed disappointment over a zero-zero finish.

Suddenly, everything made sense. Many of my days had ended in a tie. Much of my life was spent on the defense. Always in the fight, I went from challenge to challenge. Wrestling with fear and doubt, I never developed an offensive strategy to score. The rest of the time, I sat on the bench.

Standing by, I watched others play. When not playing defense or sitting on the bench, I was a spectator. Sadly, I didn't even have the opportunity to score.

Pondering how many times I had attempted progress yet failed, I was ready to change course. While I was a spectator at the soccer game, I resolved to take my position in the game of life. The time had come to play offense. I would no longer stand by passively waiting for my number to be called. Instead, I would purposefully aim for the prize.

The sunset spoke to my heart that night. Watching day turn to night gave me insight. Dusk signified the end of one day. Dawn represented hope for tomorrow. I needed to take my position, stay in the game and press forward with confidence. This would be my offensive strategy to score.

Soccer in mind, my husband and I took the kids to the field. A peaceful, Sunday afternoon made it the perfect day to play. Watching from a distance, I thought about the game of life.

At the event the day prior, my kids were spectators. On the field, they were beginners. They trained hard. Big smiles were on their faces, and they were excited to learn. Soon they would step into the game and get their chance to score.

They dared to walk on the field and had the discipline to train. Both are essential when preparing for competition. Half the battle was already won.

In the game of life, practice is vital. All must train hard in preparation. Curve balls come. Darts fly. The aim is off. All will miss the mark.

Thoughts away from the field, I reflected on my past. As a young girl, I strove for perfection. I only played if success was guaranteed. The competition was there, but I was the only player. If the possibility of failure existed, I didn't play. Unless a win was sure, the game never started.

All of a sudden, I had a vision of myself at sixteen years old at a North High track meet. Lined up, I was ready for my first race. As I nervously awaited a signal to start, I panicked inside. The track gun went off indicating the beginning of the competition.

Soaring down the track, I felt free. Exhilaration turned to disappointment when I realized I was losing. Without hesitation, I stepped off the track. That day I quit the team never to run another race.

My mind returned to the present moment, and I had a revelation. This mindset had carried into many areas of my life. Many times, I voluntarily walked off the field. Other times, I quit the pursuit before it even started.

In a soccer match, the clock ticks. Moments fall away as the end approaches. Throughout the game, the coach changes strategy and sometimes takes players off the field altogether.

In the game of life, God is our coach. Time plays the role of

My focus needed to shift away from defense. My strategy had to be set before I stepped on the field. Independent of others' reactions, I needed an offensive plan to move forward.

referee. Every game has a start and a finish. The finish is uncertain, and there is no time to waste. All must run the race with perseverance.

While I finally found the courage to step on the field, I still had my moments of doubt. At times, I stood along the sidelines. Regardless, I resolved to change my position.

If I stayed on defense, my reactions would be based on others' responses. I would stop before I started and retrace steps to get them right. I would always be one step behind. I might turn back just before I would have made it.

My focus needed to shift away from defense. My strategy had to be set before I stepped on the field. Independent of others' reactions, I needed an offensive plan to move forward.

With my husband and kids by my side, I walked off the field that beautiful, Sunday afternoon. In the distance, voice coming from the goal area, I heard my coach call. "And let us run with perseverance the race marked out for us, fixing our eyes on Jesus, the pioneer and perfecter of faith" (Hebrews 12:1-2 NIV).

————————

**IF LIFE THROWS A CURVEBALL, HANDLE IT WITH GRACE.
STEP ON THE FIELD. ADAPT AND ADJUST.
ALWAYS STAY IN THE GAME.**

————————

Julie Barbera

16 | Standing on the Inside

"So the last will be first, and the first will be last."

(Matthew 20:16 NIV)

W ould I stay down or learn to stand? Either way, I needed courage. At the core, I wanted to be accepted. It was inevitable that others would let me down. I sought external approval. Perhaps stability needed to come from within.

Every struggle came with a silver lining. I had experienced my fair share of challenges, but I was stronger because of them. They had made me who I was. And for that, I was grateful. Although I lacked strength, I mustered up enough to pick up my pen day after day. Inspired, I began to write.

Confidence in mind, I thought about my son's award ceremony the day prior. It was early morning. The sounds of buses and cars filled a crowded parking lot. Parents eagerly searched for a place to park. Many came early in anticipation of the crowd. All waited outside until the gate opened.

Once inside, parents were directed to the school cafeteria. A stage was in front, and it was lined with chairs. Waiting with expectation, I watched as fourth graders quietly filed in to take their seats.

Every student present would receive an award. Big smiles were on their faces, and all appeared to be scanning the audience. My ten-year-old son made eye contact with me, waved and then found his seat.

Once everyone was seated, the principal stood up to introduce the group. As she read from a list, the names were announced for every student who would receive the first award. My son proudly stood up, walked forward and then took his position on stage.

Students were lined up side by side. Beaming smiles brightened the room. With cameras in hand, proud parents walked forward to capture the moment.

My eyes were on the stage as I imagined students standing on the inside. Their spirits were lifted, and all were being recognized for work well done. The first group of students proudly accepted the awards and then returned to their seats.

The principal continued to read from a list. Once again, my son's name was called. He looked back to make sure that we heard and then confidently walked forward.

As I shifted my focus away from the stage, I thought about students who wouldn't receive an award that day. I imagined them waiting in half-empty classrooms. Since they were aware that their classmates were being recognized, I wondered if they were sitting down inside.

Everyone loves to be acknowledged. All of us wait with hopeful expectation for our names to be called. External awards, while gratifying, lead to a temporary sense of accomplishment. Inner strength builds the courage to stand, even when the world says sit down.

Daydreaming, my mind drifted to another place in time. I was just nine years old. While I was on the playground, my classmates laughed and played around me. Although I wasn't physically alone, I felt lonely. Lying on a grass field, I gazed up at the sky.

External rewards, while gratifying, lead to a temporary sense of accomplishment. Inner strength builds the courage to stand, even when the world says sit down.

Clouds moved in unison to form a picture. Shaped like a cup, they seemed to overlap. I imagined myself seated securely in the palm of what appeared to be a giant hand. This picture in the sky gave me comfort. Since I was lost in the moment, I didn't hear the whistle blow.

Suddenly, I awoke from a daydream. The students were lined up along the pavement. The teacher waved her arms to get my attention. I quickly jumped up and then made my way to the back of the line.

Kickball team captains were selecting players. Since I was in a daze, I didn't notice that almost all had been chosen. My heart dropped when I realized I was one among four remaining. I didn't want to be the last one standing.

Sadly, I ended up on a team by default. I was the last student to be called, so I walked to the back of the line. Although I was discouraged, I pushed through the game. Nobody seemed to notice that I was sitting down inside.

Relieved by the sound of a bell, I hurriedly made my way to the locker room. I couldn't wait to escape that ugly feeling of rejection on the playground. When it was time for lunch, I proceeded to the cafeteria.

In search of my friends, I ended up at the back of the line. When I couldn't find anyone to sit with, I resolved to sit alone. With my tray in hand, I passed a group of fifth graders. They taunted me when I walked by, and my eyes blinked rapidly as nervousness built up inside.

A secluded table on the far side of the cafeteria looked safe. While I was physically standing, I was actually sitting down inside. I couldn't wait to make it to my seat.

The afternoon was long. Although I was discouraged, I made it through. A rough day ended on a positive note. Grandma greeted me with a smile in the school parking lot. At that moment, every frozen hint of rejection melted under warmth and acceptance.

As we drove home, I looked up at the sky. I was always searching for a sign. That afternoon, I looked for clouds that had consoled me earlier in the day. And they were there. In my spirit, a hand made of fluffy clouds reached down to comfort me.

As I drifted back to the ceremony, I saw students on stage with certificates in hand. Proud parents walked forward to capture the moment. I approached my son to take a quick photo and then secure his awards. He didn't want to let them go. Respecting his wishes, I returned to my seat.

It appeared that a majority of the students had an adult there to support them. I wondered if some were alone. Maybe a few were sitting down inside, even with an award in hand.

My mind drifted once again, and I was lying on the beach. White clouds moved in unison as I looked up at the sky. I needed a sign. Whatever the case, it was there. Suddenly, I remembered that day on the playground years prior.

Crashing waves pounded the shoreline. I was sitting down inside. That day went by quickly, as all come and then drift away

CRACKED MIRROR, CLEAR REFLECTION

with the wind. With my head down, I left the beach alone. A feeling of rejection was ingrained within.

As I headed home, traffic was backed up bumper to bumper. It felt like a never-ending stretch to the exit. Relieved to have finally arrived, I waited for the light to change. Through the corner of my eye, I saw a man selling roses. Seeing flowers sparked a chain reaction in my spirit. Praying aloud, I pleaded, "God, why can't you bring someone into my life who will love me and give me flowers?"

All of a sudden, the man approached my car. He tapped on my window and pointed to the flowers. Although apprehensive, I rolled my window down. He said, "Ma'am, these flowers are for you." Gazing at the roses in awe, I asked, "Who gave them to me?" He responded, "Ma'am, someone just wanted to give you flowers."

As I quickly counted the roses, I was amazed to find that there were seven. At that moment, rejection's ice cold grip melted under unconditional love. In my spirit, I heard: "You did not choose me, but I chose you and appointed you so that you might go and bear fruit—fruit that will last—and so that whatever you ask in my name the Father will give you" (John 15:16 NIV).

Learning to stand inside, with or without recognition, would give my son the courage to fulfill his God-given purpose.

Throughout childhood and into adulthood, I lacked the courage to press through resistance and judgment. I went through my share of highs and lows. Although there were moments when I was on the mountaintop, what stood out were the many times I sat in the valley.

While I still doubted and got down on myself at times, I

didn't stay down. Acceptance from others was important, but it wasn't everything. I needed to believe in myself first. Inner strength would give me the courage to stand.

Back at the ceremony, my son walked forward to receive his third award. I was confident he was standing up inside. If he wasn't, I was standing for him.

At that moment, I resolved to teach the real meaning of courage. External awards, while significant, are fleeting. Learning to stand inside, with or without recognition, would give my son the courage to fulfill his God-given purpose.

God spoke to my heart in a small, school cafeteria that morning. The last few names were read. After a moment of silence, my name was called. As I stood up inside, I was reminded of my true source of strength. "For I know the plans I have for you," declares the Lord, "plans to prosper you and not to harm you, plans to give you hope and a future" (Jeremiah 29:11 NIV).

STAND, EVEN IF THE WORLD SAYS SIT DOWN.
DON'T SEEK APPROVAL. PURSUE PURPOSE.

SOCIETY TELLS US WE NEED TO FIT IN.
IF WE WANT TO FULFILL OUR POTENTIAL,
WE MUST LEARN TO STAND OUT.

Julie Barbera

17 | Hold on Tightly

"So do not fear, for I am with you; do not be
dismayed, for I am your God. I will strengthen you
and help you; I will uphold you with my righteous
right hand."

(Isaiah 41:10 NIV)

Would I move forward or let fear hold me back? Either
way, tomorrow would come. The future was uncertain,
and the unknown loomed in the distance. I had a choice: walk by
faith or run and hide. Perhaps I just needed to hold on tightly.

In the park with family, I visualized a brighter tomorrow. In
many ways, I lived the life I had once imagined. The past was the
past. I couldn't stay there, but it helped to reflect.

Uncertainty had once paralyzed me. Meeting the right man had once felt impossible. I was even told I wouldn't be able to have children. While I had come a long way, I aspired to go further.

On a long-awaited journey, it took years to find the courage to step out. My mission was to use my gifts and talents to encourage others. I wanted to love the life I was living and live with purpose. Yet, my vision seemed like nothing more than just an empty dream.

A better future wasn't just a dream. It was a reality. The family in front of me was proof. Even so, I felt like something was missing. I wanted to do more, have more and be more.

My faith had been tested, and I had faced challenges along the way. God had shown up time and time again. Although He had proven Himself faithful, I still doubted.

As usual, my day started early. Darkness met sunlight with a cup of coffee. Clarity allowed for deeper reflection, and I needed a dash of hope. An afternoon at the park was my inspiration. With my pen in hand, I began to write.

I was distracted by taking pictures, and I had fallen behind. My sons darted across a field passing a soccer ball back and forth. My younger son stole the ball from his brother and then kicked it into the goal. My husband stayed close to them. I watched from the sidelines and then snapped a picture in my mind.

Suddenly, I was reminded of an experience that I hadn't thought about for years. As my attention shifted away from the field, I went back in time. My best friend and I were immersed in conversation as we headed back to Hagerstown after an evening out.

I had gone home for a few days to get away from my worries in Florida. Since I already struggled with trust, it didn't help that I had recently passed through a series of relationship issues. It felt like I would spend the rest of my life alone, and I was convinced that God had forgotten about me.

At close to midnight, we had just left Baltimore. Surrounded by woods, we found ourselves on a lonely stretch of highway with no exit for miles. A few trucks sporadically passed. All of a sudden, we were the only car on the road. We picked up speed on a downward slope, and then our car shook as we made our way around a curve.

Our full attention shifted to the road when the car slowed down. I thought my friend put on the brakes intentionally, but I quickly realized we were in trouble. We made our way to the median and then abruptly came to a stop. Weak puttering sounds shifted to silence. The only sound inside the car was a clicking noise as she desperately tried to restart the engine.

Fenced in by the obscurity of the woods, we sat in silence. Dim headlights provided a little light. We were barely off the road, and our car vibrated as a large truck passed. Desperate thoughts came to mind when I realized that our options were limited. I imagined hiding in the woods or crawling into the trunk of the car until morning.

Since we were on an infrequently traveled stretch of highway, no cars were in sight. Neither of us had a cell phone to call for help. And the hope of a police officer coming to the rescue quickly diminished.

Our hearts pounded and fear welled up inside. Prompted to pray, we bowed our heads. "God will send someone," I stated. "He has to send someone." When I prayed aloud, scripture dominated my thoughts. "For God has not given us a spirit of fear, but of power and of love and of a sound mind" (2 Timothy 1:7 NKJV).

Then God spoke to my heart, *Get out of the car now and walk.* Once again, a scripture rolled through my mind. "For God has not given us a spirit of fear, but of power and of love and of a sound mind" (2 Timothy 1:7 NKJV). Repeating these words over and over, a feeling of peace came over me. Our car's headlights grew dimmer by the second. Again I heard, *Get out of the car now and walk.* Only this time I heard, *Hold her hand.*

I turned to my friend and shared what I felt that we were supposed to do. She questioned what I was saying, but she trusted that what I said was true. While getting out of the car made no sense in the natural, it made perfect sense spiritually. Again I heard, *Get out of the car now and walk. Hold her hand.*

We finally listened and got out of the car. My heart was pounding, and my knees were shaking. I set one foot in front of the other and took a step. As I looked back, the headlights had faded entirely. Hand in hand, we walked down a lonely stretch of highway. We had no idea where we were going since there was no exit for miles. At that moment, all trust was in God.

Hand in hand, we walked down a lonely stretch of highway. We had no idea where we were going since there was no exit for miles. At that moment, all trust was in God.

All of a sudden, I spotted two bright lights in the distance. The hope of rescue was accompanied by fear when I saw the silhouette of a person walking toward us. Pausing for a moment, I contemplated running back to the car.

My friend stopped and questioned, "Are you sure that God told us to get out of the car?" I quickly stated, "Yes, keep walking. He said that He would send someone." Words of faith gave me strength as they dominated my thoughts. "For God has not given us a spirit of fear, but of power and of love and of a sound mind" (2 Timothy 1:7 NKJV).

As we walked closer, I made out the image of a man. Hesitating for just a second, my instincts told me to run back to the car and hide. But this was no longer a viable option.

Calling out from a distance, the man spoke, "It's okay, I am here to help." Close enough to see the stranger's face, I hesitated. Speaking in a calm voice, he said, "You got out of the car at just the right time. There was only one spot that was safe enough to pull over. Had you not gotten out of the car exactly when you did, I wouldn't have stopped. In fact, I almost didn't stop. But when I saw you holding hands, I knew you were in trouble."

The kind man offered to drive us to my friend's grandparents' house ten miles away. By the grace of God, we arrived safe and sound. It wasn't a pattern to trust strangers, especially on a dark road in the middle of the night. In this case, we chose to walk by faith.

God sent an angel to rescue us that night. Before this incident, I felt forgotten. I quickly dismissed that thought. All problems seemed to shrink in comparison to the grace that I sensed at that moment. I thought to myself, *If I can trust God with my life, I can trust Him with my relationships.*

Uncertainty loomed. My first response was to run and hide. Trust gave me the courage to move forward and hold on tightly.

Thinking back, I realize how invaluable this experience was in my life. Uncertainty loomed. My first response was to run and hide. Trust gave me the courage to move forward and hold on tightly.

Since soccer practice was over for my sons, my family was resting on a nearby bench. I walked across the field to join them. Having spent time reflecting, I had missed out on an excellent opportunity to share. There was no sense looking back. I resolved to take advantage of opportunities in the future.

For years, I stood on the sidelines. Trust was a struggle. Building courage was close to impossible. Afraid of making mistakes, I failed to move forward.

Caught up in pursuing dreams, many had already come to pass. The blessings before my eyes were proof. Hand in hand, I walked off the field with my family.

Yes, I still doubted at times. Although the fear of the unknown was there, it didn't hold me back. God stood by. He was ready to meet me. I just needed to hold on tightly.

Looking up at the clouds, I spotted a familiar sight. They formed what looked like a giant hand. As I made out a picture in the sky, I was comforted by a message. "Fear not, for I *am* with you; Be not dismayed, for I *am* your God. I will strengthen you, Yes, I will help you, I will uphold you with My righteous right hand" (Isaiah 41:10 NKJV).

———

IF LIFE TAKES YOU DOWN A ROUGH ROAD, HOLD ON TIGHT.
YOU'LL GET THROUGH THE RIDE, STRONGER THAN BEFORE.

IF YOU FORGET HOW FAR YOU'VE COME, REFLECT.
ADJUST THE REARVIEW MIRROR.
KEEP YOUR EYES ON THE ROAD AHEAD.

———

Julie Barbera

18 | Molded Like Clay

"Yet you, Lord, are our father.
We are the clay, you are the potter;
we are all the work of your hand."

(Isaiah 64:8 NIV)

W ould I resist being shaped or accept change with grace? Either way, change in life was inevitable. Like clay on a wheel, I was molded. Squeezed and pressed on every side, only God knew what I would become. Nicks, scratches and flaws were the results. And perhaps they would be used for His glory.

Growth came when stretched. Unknowns involved risk. I stuck with what I knew. I understood the value of change, but I tended to resist it even when for my own good. The more I resisted, the more I stressed.

Life was about resilience. Lessons came from experience, and I learned from my mistakes. Even so, I stayed within my comfort zone. I wrote to break the mold. In search of a breakthrough, I merely dabbled with risk. Not sure where to start, I picked up my pen to write.

It was Saturday morning. I was just ten years old, and I gazed out the back window. Oak trees dressed in autumn colors lined the streets. Birds soared high in the sky.

Growth came when stretched. Unknowns involved risk. I stuck with what I knew. I understood the value of change, but I tended to resist it even when for my own good.

Grandma and I were headed to an art workshop at the local museum. The class was usually full. We were behind. Since I was shy, I didn't like to show up late. While I didn't want to go that day, I still visualized what I would create.

We arrived at the park and then made our way down a long road. The museum was nestled on a cul-de-sac, and autumn leaves covered the ground. Shaded by oak trees, we pulled into a crowded parking lot. Although I was nervous that the class had already started, I mustered up the courage to go inside.

We got out of the car in a rush. The wind whistled, and dry leaves crunched underfoot. Step by step, we climbed a wide set of stairs. The door was locked, so we rang the bell. An attendant buzzed us inside. Thankfully, the nervous feeling I felt in the car had gone away.

The attendant instructed us to follow her. We were directed through rooms full of paintings and sculptures, and the artwork was a pleasant distraction. Led down a dimly lit hallway, we arrived at our destination. As expected, the class was packed.

A pottery wheel was in front. Tables and chairs filled the room. Students watched as the potter demonstrated how to reshape a gray slab of clay. As the machine was spinning, expert hands assisted. A large lump of clay slowly took form.

With his hands in synchrony with the wheel, the potter created what appeared to be a flawless work of art. Starting out as a lump, the clay was molded into a perfectly symmetrical pot. Since the clay pot was ready for firing, it was placed in a kiln.

Directed to put on a smock, I grabbed a piece of clay and made my way to a table in the back of the room. As I looked out a small window, I thought about what I would create. Clay in hand with no idea what to make, I rolled it on the table.

All of a sudden, the potter stood up to make an announcement. Students were told to create a bowl. Relieved to finally have direction, I prepared for the formation of my masterpiece.

Watching intently, others flattened out lumps of clay. Using palms to apply pressure, I followed their lead. The potter then directed all to form a ball. My piece, now wholly flat, was soft enough for shaping. Once again, I rolled it under the palm of my hand.

In front of the class, the potter demonstrated how to turn a ball of clay into a usable vessel. Pinching edges with thumbs centered, he carved out the inside. Focused on stability, he flattened out the bottom. Lines and ridges made his creation unique. Using specialized tools, the bowl was decorated with care. A gray lump of clay was thoughtfully transformed.

Before we began, the potter encouraged students to come to the front of the room to examine his work. I shyly walked forward. As I looked closely, I noticed nicks and scratches. Although well-formed, the outer surface wasn't as smooth as expected. From afar, I was unable to see imperfections. Up close, they were visible yet acceptable.

After doing as the potter had instructed, I returned to my seat. I quickly glanced at the small piece of clay in front of me. Since I was ready to try, I did precisely as he had demonstrated. As I squeezed over and over, close attention was paid to detail. With my thumbs centered, I pinched the clay to form edges.

When I looked down, I noticed many imperfections. No matter how many times I went over my work, it was impossible to create a perfectly shaped bowl. Using my fingers, I tried to smooth out the surface. Despite my efforts, flaws were visible.

Comparing my bowl to the potter's vessel, mine lacked definition. Although unique in appearance and usable by design, his creation was much more refined. Still, mine had character. I took a step back to admire my work. Up close, imperfections were noticeable. From a distance, I saw a treasured piece of art.

Immersed in thought, I was startled when Grandma came from behind to admire my handiwork. I am sure that she saw flaws, yet she made no mention of them.

Since I was directed to place my bowl on a table, I walked across the room. With a masterpiece in hand, I handled it with care. I wanted to paint, but the clay needed time to dry. The potter reassured the class that we would finish the following week.

Students shuffled around. The room was almost empty as Grandma and I made our way to the door. As we exited the museum, I admired others' work. Still, I couldn't stop thinking about what my creation would become.

Leaves crunched underfoot, and the wind whistled in my ears as we walked toward the car. I was making big plans for my vessel. When I visualized the final product, imperfections no longer mattered. As I imagined brilliant color and design, a small lump of clay was shaped in my mind.

We drove down a long lane, and beauty surrounded us on both sides. I gazed at a line of oak trees decorated in autumn colors. I was ten years old with a lifetime of lessons to be learned. If for just a moment in time, everything made sense.

Many years later, I remembered that day at the museum. Wanting to create special memories with my sons, I longed to share what a small lump of clay had taught me years prior.

I was close to home, and a few hours were left in the day. My family and I decided to stop at the craft store. With memories of the museum fresh in mind, I made my way down a dimly lit aisle.

An assortment of clay filled the shelves. Tools for shaping and design covered the walls. Since there was so much variety to choose from, I had no idea where to begin. Alone in the aisle, I gazed at blocks of clay.

After selecting the proper clay, I picked up tools for shaping. The right paint was chosen to add finishing touches. Since the kids were excited to go home and start, I hurriedly made my way to the register to pay.

Finally home, my children waited at the table. I placed a small lump of clay in front of each of them. Both looked down in wonder. Never having worked with real clay, they had no idea where to begin.

With a lump of clay in hand, I demonstrated what the potter had taught me years prior. I rolled a piece under the palm of my hand and then created a ball. Since I was older now, working with clay was easier. My children, on the other hand, struggled to soften the clay enough for shaping.

In synchrony, we pinched and squeezed. With our thumbs inside, we carved out the center and then molded the sides. Focused on creativity, small lumps of clay were changed. As we smoothed out the surface, our concentration shifted to curves. Tiny patterns and ridges added character.

My older son and I paid close attention to detail in an attempt to make our work unique. My younger son had almost given up. Although he had exerted tremendous effort, he ended up with a lopsided bowl. Frustrated, he placed it in front of me and walked away.

Suddenly, my focus shifted to my son's misshapen bowl. It was close to falling apart. Unstable, it began to crumble. I had to act fast. Back to the basics, I squeezed the clay to form a ball and then started the reshaping process. Molded with care, a malformed lump of clay turned into a work of art.

As I stepped back to admire my creation, the transformed vessel seemed to speak; "Shall what is formed say to the one who formed it, 'Why did you make me like this?' Does not the potter have the right to make out of the same lump of clay some pottery for special purposes and some for common use?" (Romans 9:20-21 NIV). Like the lump of clay, I needed to remain pliable in God's hands.

My son had demonstrated courage by trying, and he was willing to admit that he needed help. By remaining flexible, he allowed me to reshape the clay as I saw fit. Though he was just a young child, he had exhibited character that I sometimes lacked. Afraid of making mistakes, I didn't even start. In pursuit of perfection, I resisted reshaping even when for my own good.

Change can be painful, especially when pulled in many directions. Resistance leads to more bumps and scratches. Surrendering to molding and shaping enables God to change us. This leads to a smoother transition into who He has called us to be.

Gazing at the changed vessel, I saw small defects. Surprisingly, it was imperfections that gave the bowl character. Reminded of that autumn morning at the museum, I shared a profound lesson captured by the innocent mind of a child. I wanted my work to turn out like that of the potter. The potter's creation looked perfect from a distance, yet flaws were visible up close. In reality, it was all about my perception.

Despite my tendency to resist change, I was able to look beyond nicks and scratches. Squeezed and pressed on every side, the process was painful. Even so, it didn't break me.

Although I still had flaws, I viewed them as evidence of growth. Grace had changed me, and for that I was grateful. All would be used for God's glory. And I no longer tried to hide cracks.

Nicks and scratches make work unique, and this brings out its character. Perfection is just an illusion. All have cracks and blemishes. Even the tiniest lump of clay can be transformed into a treasured masterpiece.

Although I still had flaws, I viewed them as evidence of growth. Grace had changed me, and for that I was grateful.

Now that I was forty years old with many lessons yet to be learned, if for just a moment in time, all made sense. As I gazed at treasures before me, some shaped with small hands and others formed by mighty hands, God spoke to my heart through a small lump of clay. "But we have this treasure in jars of clay to show that this all-surpassing power is from God and not from us" (2 Corinthians 4:7 NIV).

LIKE CLAY ON A WHEEL, ALL GO THROUGH
STAGES OF MOLDING AND SHAPING.
SQUEEZED AND PRESSED ON EVERY SIDE,
ONLY GOD KNOWS WHAT YOU'LL BECOME.

CIRCUMSTANCES DON'T DEFINE YOU. THEY SHAPE YOU.
YOU'RE MOLDED TO MAKE A DIFFERENCE.
LET YOUR LIGHT SHINE BRIGHTLY, EVEN THROUGH THE CRACKS.

Julie Barbera

19 | Strength in Weakness

"My grace is sufficient for you,
for my power is made perfect in weakness."

(2 Corinthians 12:9 NIV)

W ould weakness stop me or would I find strength in
weakness? Either way, I wasn't willing to give up. Like
an unfinished clay vessel, I sat on the shelf waiting for the perfect
timing. Perhaps my moment had already come.

My motivation wasn't enough. It prompted action, but it only
took me so far. It wasn't hard to start. The challenge was to finish
what I had started, and my manuscript was no exception.

My morning routine kept me consistent. With my Bible and a
notebook by my side, I woke up early to put pen to paper. While I

moved forward in some ways, I stood still in many others. The mere act of writing felt safe. The risk would come later. In deep thought, I began to write.

Months went by with no progress. The clay bowls my sons and I had created sat on the shelf. Half finished, they awaited the last stages of completion. In need of paint and gloss, they lacked the beauty of a finished product.

They had been molded with care, and we had big plans for what they would become. Time had been spent pinching and squeezing the pieces into their final form. Great attention had been paid to detail. Days had gone by as we waited for the clay to dry. All had been done in anticipation of putting on the finishing touches.

Covered with paint and then topped with a shiny coat, the bowls were supposed to be complete. As I thought about the final product, I imagined refined vessels. Instead, they sat on a shelf wrapped in aluminum foil. Maybe they had been covered to prevent crumbling. Perhaps I had preserved them for another day. Although they had been forgotten for a season, their appearance was just as unique as the day they were created.

As I gazed at our handiwork, I resolved to finish what had been started months prior. *Not now,* I thought, wrapping them once again and placing them back on the shelf. *Soon, very soon, just not today.* With so much going on, I wasn't quite ready. It was best to wait for the right timing, and all had to be in order.

This was a weakness of mine: starting things without finishing and living with unfulfilled dreams. I was never quite ready to take a leap of faith. Since I relied on approval for worth, I lacked the courage to walk in grace. I sat on a shelf of self-inflicted perfectionism.

When I reflected on seasons of shaping, I saw myself as an unfinished vessel. Still, God's grace was evident despite my imperfections. Although I wanted to pursue dreams, idealistic standards always seemed to stop me. I saw a reflection of my life in small bowls made of clay.

As I focused on half-finished vessels wrapped in foil, I was reminded: "My grace is sufficient for you, for my power is made perfect in weakness" (2 Corinthians 12:9 NIV).

Since I was trapped in a vicious cycle of unrealistic expectations, I took responsibility for things that were out of my control. This somehow made me feel in control. Starting over made it easier to cope with confusion. If I could start again with more clarity, all would fall into place. That was the hope.

Setting high standards was a way of dealing with the world. If only I were a better version of myself, my problems would somehow be solved. Self-esteem centered around appearance. Striving for perfection gave me the hope of one day having worth. That was my dream.

Attention shifted back to unfinished clay bowls. I heard the sound of my children's voices. "Mom, let's finish the clay. When can we paint the bowls?" "Not yet," I said, "Later, we can finish them later." Pushing things off to another day and waiting for the ideal moment, that was my pattern.

Once again, I reflected on my life. While I had spent years chasing after mirages of perfection, I was ready to put the past behind to follow God's plan. It was clear that much time had already been wasted.

Since I was ready to add the finishing touches, I removed the clay pieces from the ledge. I thoughtfully unwrapped them and then placed them on the table. It was time to begin.

Eager to start, my children called out in excitement, "Mom, can we paint the clay now? Please, we want to paint." As I responded with action, I prepared a work area. Paint and paintbrushes were in the center of the table. An unfinished clay bowl was placed in front of each of them. I set one in front of myself as well.

As I visualized the final product, I picked up my paintbrush.

Present in the moment, the truth was revealed. A clear connection was made between myself and a small bowl made of clay.

For years, I had a vision of God's plan. Rather than pursue it, I did nothing. Neatly seated on the shelf, I lacked the courage to take a chance. I kept myself busy to avoid feeling empty. Perfectionism filled a void yet stopped forward progress.

Focusing on improvement led to a false sense of control. Even when ready, I feared failure so much that I chose to do nothing. I needed to make a decision to do something. Accepting myself unconditionally would lead to true freedom.

Like the clay bowl, I was molded and shaped. On the outside, I appeared ready. Inside, I was afraid of being wrong. Fear ultimately stopped me from moving forward.

When I looked closely at my bowl, it had lots of nicks and scratches. Even so, it was special in my eyes. I wondered if God saw me the same way. All along I thought that imperfections made me unworthy of His plan. But it was these flaws that would be used for His glory.

Although I had vulnerabilities and shortcomings, God's power was evident during times of weakness. Molded and shaped, at times stretched, I saw myself like clay in His hands. Pride needed to be overcome. Humbled under God's mighty hand, I needed to rely on His strength alone. Grace was the answer.

Creating bowls and sitting them on the shelf was a way of revealing the truth. Maybe I was afraid of making mistakes. Perhaps I thought that they would be irreversible. Whatever the case, it was time to get off the shelf and take a chance.

Pride needed to be overcome. Humbled under God's mighty hand, I needed to rely on His strength alone. Grace was the answer.

Finished bowls were placed on the windowsill. A light shone through making it easy to see cracks and blemishes. Although the flaws were readily visible, my perception was unaltered. As I admired refined yet imperfect works of art, words of truth reminded me of my real source of strength. "Therefore I will boast all the more gladly about my weaknesses, so that Christ's power may rest on me. That is why, for Christ's sake, I delight in weaknesses, in insults, in hardships, in persecutions, in difficulties. For when I am weak, then I am strong" (2 Corinthians 12:9-10 NIV).

LIKE UNFINISHED CLAY VESSELS,
MANY SIT ON A SHELF WAITING FOR PERFECT TIMING.

PERFECTION IS JUST AN ILLUSION.
ALL HAVE CRACKS AND BLEMISHES.
EVEN THE TINIEST LUMP OF CLAY CAN BE TRANSFORMED
INTO A TREASURED MASTERPIECE.

Julie Barbera

20 | Mustard Seed Faith

"Now faith is the substance of things hoped for,
the evidence of things not seen."

(Hebrews 11:1 NKJV)

W ould I stay back or stand out? Either way, there was some risk. Determined to step on stage, I stood behind the curtain. Since I wasn't quite ready for the spotlight, I played it safe. Authenticity was key. Perhaps I just needed the courage to be me.

Like a clay bowl on the shelf, I stood by. With every dab of paint, the pottery was transformed. In the same way, every step forward turned my vision into reality.

As usual, my morning started with reflection. Creativity

usually flowed freely, but this day was different. I searched for answers. With the hope that inspiration would find me, I began to write.

While a path was laid out and the way seemed clear, I was only able to make it so far. Every attempt to move forward resulted in a roadblock. Something was standing in my way. Spinning in circles like a cat chasing its tail, I pursued a moving target. Many days, although full, were empty. And doubt crept in to stop progress.

When I was controlled by fear, it was hard to walk by faith. Fear was contrary to faith. I saw it as the substance of things dreaded, the anticipation of things that hadn't happened yet. Many things feared had never happened, nor would they ever occur.

Operating in faith would leave no room for fear to reside. With faith as a shield, fear and doubt wouldn't penetrate. Like an arrow hitting a suit of armor, they would simply bounce off.

Now that I had my vision in sight, stepping out came with risk. A wrong turn could potentially lead to failure. Success as the only acceptable result left me defeated before I even started. A willingness to accept the outcome, good or bad, gave me the courage to take a chance.

All of a sudden, I was reminded of the bowl I had just finished. It would soon be ready for the stand. I kept it on the windowsill since the paint still needed time to dry. The sun shined through the window making it easy to see cracks and blemishes. With the bowl's flaws readily visible, uncertainty set in. Then, an all too familiar thought came to mind. *Maybe I should start over. Perhaps I should try again.*

In pursuit of perfection, I was no stranger to starting over. Having something to perfect, change or redo made it acceptable to passively stand by. Essentially, it was easy to justify doing nothing.

Since the paint was finally dry, the finished bowl was ready for display. The perfect spot would provide both visibility and safety. Authenticity left it vulnerable. Putting it anywhere in the spotlight involved risk.

Suddenly, everything made sense. Like the bowl, I attempted to step out with minimal risk. I longed for visibility yet held on to security. Going in circles while standing still, I ended up in the same spot.

With the bowl's flaws readily visible, uncertainty set in. Then, an all too familiar thought came to mind. *Maybe I should start over. Perhaps I should try again.*

Idealistic thinking stopped me from trying. Steps of faith enabled me to push through barriers. Recognizing that circumstances would never be perfect gave me the courage to step out.

At times, I walked boldly. Other times, I held on to faith as small as a mustard seed. Either way, I had faith. Little mustard seeds represent the slightest glimmer of hope. Yet under the right conditions, they grow. Independent of me, faith had the power to turn what seemed impossible into a reality.

A decision needed to be made: to live in fear or walk by faith. One thing was perfectly clear; challenges would no longer stop me. I would focus on what I could do and celebrate small accomplishments along the way.

Although I still stood back at times, I was determined to stand out. While I wasn't quite ready to step on stage, the curtain was open. But courage didn't come by playing it safe. It came by stepping out.

Looking up at the high mountain, the impossible suddenly felt within reach. My sights were set on the vision ahead. Despite my doubts, I put one foot in front of the other and walked by faith.

I thoughtfully removed my bowl from the shelf and then set it on the stand. It wasn't quite ready for the spotlight, so I pushed it to the back. Nestled in the corner, it was safe.

I walked away and then turned around to make a minor adjustment. The bowl was all the way in the back. I pushed it forward just a tad. It was still in the corner, only now it was closer. Since the room was dark, I turned on the lights. Then, I was reminded of the truth. "Truly I tell you, if you have faith as small as a mustard seed, you can say to this mountain, 'Move from here to there,' and it will move. Nothing will be impossible for you" (Matthew 17:20 NIV).

———

STEP INTO WHAT YOU'RE MEANT TO DO,
AND YOU'LL BECOME ALL THAT YOU'RE CALLED TO BE.

CONSISTENCY IS KEY. PICK UP ONE ROCK A DAY.
ONE DAY YOU'LL LOOK BACK AND REALIZE YOU MOVED A MOUNTAIN.

———

Julie Barbera

21 | Unguarded

"I can do all things through Christ
who strengthens me."

(Philippians 4:13 NKJV)

Was I held together with substance or would stress lead to cracks? Either way, challenges would come. Life was full of highs and lows. Pressure couldn't be avoided. Despite my willingness to persist, I needed the strength not to quit.

Everyday life felt meaningless. I was determined to find a purpose. While I knew what to do, I lacked the courage to do it. I understood in my mind but needed to believe in my heart.

In search of direction, I was inspired to write. Putting thoughts on paper was a way to connect. Clarity brought the truth to light. Creativity made the truth easier to accept, and discipline kept me going.

It wasn't hard to start writing my book, but it was undoubtedly hard to finish. I set out with good intentions. Efforts quickly turned to frustration when things didn't go as expected. A tendency to doubt made it hard for me to get things done. I hoped that my manuscript would be the exception and not the rule.

And a piece of clay molded with my hands helped to shape my thoughts.

Pen in hand, I searched for answers. They were closer to the surface than I thought. Writing made them easier to see. And a piece of clay molded with my hands helped to shape my thoughts.

My kids and I had recently purchased clay for fun. The goal was to make something simple. It was never our intention to create refined pottery. Although we didn't have the right equipment or experience, the real lesson came by trying.

Our bowls weren't made with high-quality material. We bought inexpensive clay from a local craft store. They weren't molded with a potter's hands. Our amateur hands shaped them.

My clay creation would be ready one day. Awaiting the right moment, it sat on the shelf. My kids convinced me to put it on a stand in the family room. Since my creation wasn't ready for the spotlight, I had found the perfect place tucked in a corner.

It had charm, but outer beauty wasn't enough. True strength would be measured by its ability to endure trials. At the core, it was a bowl. Nothing could change what it was created to be. *But would it last?*

Temperatures would change. Stress would come and go. Heat would cause it to stretch, and cold would lead to cracks. Over time, the color would fade. Perfectly rounded edges would chip and break. Yet if held together with substance, it would stay intact.

Transparency brought the truth to light, and contrast made the message clear. The new bowl wasn't alone on the stand. It sat beside an older piece of pottery. Surprisingly, I saw aspects of myself in both.

Worn yet refined, the aged piece demonstrated subtle charm. Quality material held it together. A solid base made it stable. Above all else, the core was its strength. Like the older pottery, I had gone through years of testing. With time, I had built the fortitude to stand.

When the bowl was filled to overflowing, it felt useful. Whether filled to the brim or barren, it had the same value. With abundance came joy. Emptiness led to dismay. It stood firm through highs and lows, as it was created to endure extremes.

Years passed. External beauty began to fade, and it lacked shine. Even so, it exhibited character that only developed with time. Faded paint made the older piece stand out. Yet, it looked worn beside newer pottery.

In reality, the more modern piece hadn't yet endured the same highs and lows. External beauty would only take it so far. Its full potential would never be reached playing it safe, securely hiding on the stand. It would fulfill its real purpose by risking brokenness.

At times, the stand was crowded. Other times, the bowl was pushed to the side. When it was close to falling off, firm footing kept it in place.

The bowl was not just made to take in. It was created to pour out. Through giving, it found real significance.

Focused on the older pottery's authenticity, I questioned myself. *Would I stay strong through highs and lows? Would I find the courage to stand for something greater than myself?*

Comparing myself to a worn bowl made of clay forced me to examine my heart. By questioning what I was truly made of, areas of weakness were exposed. Like the new bowl, my strength was superficial. My worth existed merely in my external features, and this led to self-doubt.

The newer bowl somehow looked different. In fact, it appeared sturdier than ever beside the worn bowl. Yet something substantial was missing; it lacked substance. It held on to a brilliant shine of youth. A fresh, modern look gave it vitality. But grace would only be revealed through trials. Strength would be proven by the test of time.

Just like the finished clay, I had weaknesses. I may have looked together on the outside, but I was far from flawless. An inability to accept shortcomings didn't make me stronger. It actually made me weaker.

Like a puppet in a marionette show, I danced for others but fear kept my hands tied.

An appearance of strength may have fooled others, but I could only fool myself for so long. I looked together on the outside. Like a puppet in a marionette show, I danced for others but fear kept my hands tied.

Like the clay bowl's exterior, my outside appearance would eventually fade. Reliance on the superficial would only take me so far. Just as a strong core gave the bowl stability, I needed inner strength to stand for something greater than myself.

Since I was no longer operating with an expectation of flawlessness, I was able to accept strengths and weaknesses alike. Guarding my heart was part of the journey, and it needed to become a way of life.

Although pressure still left cracks at times, this was something I needed to accept. Stress was a part of life. Highs and lows would come. They simply couldn't be avoided.

It was essential to build strength from the inside out, not from the outside in. This would develop my character. And true substance would give me the courage to stand the test of time.

As I stepped away from the stand, the bowl's purpose was clear. It didn't have a voice, but it spoke clearly through silence. "Above all else, guard your heart, for everything you do flows from it" (Proverbs 4:23 NIV).

LIFE INVOLVES RISK. OTHERS MAY JUDGE.
LEARN TO STAND, EVEN WHEN TOLD TO SIT DOWN.
TRUE STRENGTH IS INSIDE. THIS IS YOUR SAFE PLACE.

Julie Barbera

22 | An Illusion of Order

"I am the Lord your God,
who teaches you what is best for you,
who directs you in the way you should go."

(Isaiah 48:17 NIV)

W ould order lead to balance or was balance the path to order? Either way, life was a balancing act. I went from erasing mistakes to rewriting parts of my story. The pursuit was perfection, and it seemed I would never arrive.

My idea of order centered around control. I wasn't ready to accept that many things were simply beyond my control. My definition was flawed and needed to change.

The desire to write this book was no different than any other.

I had a goal that I was bound and determined to achieve. I was the captain of the ship and steered it where I wished. But not so fast. It was soon evident that the book was leading me, not the other way around.

God was the captain of the ship. I had a pen in hand, and He held a pencil at the captain's log. Away from the ship's wheel, I was a passenger along for the ride. *When would I get there, and how would I arrive?* These answers were yet to be determined. What was certain is that I would get to my destination.

At the start of my journey, I lost my voice for a short period. Unable to talk, I was forced to listen. Listening made life easier to understand. Understanding allowed me to confront the truth. Confronting the truth enabled me to face things that were out of my control and to accept the unchangeable.

My voice was my paintbrush. It was my greatest asset: my tool of choice. I dreamed of one day using it to motivate others. Unable to speak for a season, I was forced to lay it down. Indeed, I couldn't paint a picture without a brush.

Although self-expression was my greatest obstacle, other tools didn't seem to have the same value. A strong desire to express thoughts made it hard to hear over them. I spoke more than I listened. I failed to pay close attention. Consequently, my picture ended up blurred.

Unable to speak, I started to write. Forced to listen, I began to comprehend. It was no longer a goal to speak my mind. Instead, I sought to understand what affected my mindset. Once I knew the answer, I would be ready to talk.

Before laying my brush down, I tried to paint the perfect picture of my life. The flexibility to cover the canvas was liberating for a season. The ability to use a paintbrush of choice made me feel in control. Even so, true freedom would only come by letting go.

Set aside for a season, my paintbrush was neatly tucked away.

Laid down but not forgotten, it would be lifted in due time. Tempted to pick it up once again, I consciously resisted the urge.

Vocal expression was on hold until my final draft was complete. The number of revisions I attempted could only be calculated by counting the dulling pencils in my art box. I was uncertain as to how many drafts would be written. The number was unknown. Time would tell.

In search of the right pen to write my manuscript, I opened my art box. It was full of useful tools, yet it was uncrowded. Eyes to see and ears to hear were securely tucked away in a corner. Still, it was hard to look past the blur of dark paint that covered an unfinished canvas.

As expected, my box was full of pencils, and most were dull. I found a sharp pencil and a ballpoint pen, and both were at the bottom of the box. Other tools were pushed to the side.

Many pencils were broken, and the ones with tips were blunt. Every pencil had an eraser, but overuse made most of no use at all. It was necessary to press hard to write and to bear down to erase. Worthless erasers no longer erased mistakes. Instead, they left dark smudges behind.

Small pieces of crumbled up paper were scattered throughout the box. I opened just a few. It was evident that much effort had gone into rewriting parts of the story. Familiar words jumped off of torn pages. Thoroughly acquainted with every detail, I was reading my own manuscript.

Yes, crumbling up used paper was a pattern. It carried into every area of my life. My soon-to-be-published book was no exception. I started and stopped, made changes then started again. In the end, I found myself in the same spot.

My goal was to make a difference. I wanted to do something significant. The misconception was that all needed to be in order. The minute one thing was resolved, something else came up.

Order turned to chaos, and then chaos returned to peace. I was always close to ready, but then the next thing popped up, and the cycle continued. It didn't seem that real order was even possible, at least not my definition. So, I chose to wait.

For years, I had considered writing a book. It was part of the vision. The timing seemed right, but there was no guarantee. I was carefully positioned in what I thought was the right spot, only to find that there was no perfect place or time. With one finger on the hold button, I paused my writing for a season. Sadly, I went back to square one.

At times, I chose logic over faith. Thus, pencils quickly shifted from sharp to dull. In an attempt to erase mistakes, I grabbed pencils out of God's hand. It was soon evident that rewriting the story and trying to erase the errors on my own were futile tasks.

Ripped paper and smudge marks were the results of my wasted effort. The harder I pushed, the darker the marks I left behind me. Many words were still legible, yet they were torn and covered with streaks.

Dull pencils and used paintbrushes made it challenging to write. But something felt different this time. With a blunt pencil in hand, I longed to pick up my pen once again.

I suddenly spotted a large eraser in the corner. Worn out from use, it appeared someone had tried to erase pen. Pen marks were impossible to eliminate. Some things could not be so easily undone. I turned to God and asked, "Why is there an eraser if I can only write with a pen?" He responded, "That is the eraser I have been using to purify your heart. I have had to erase and rewrite many of your stories to show that I was with you all along."

Writing without an eraser felt risky, but God would be beside me with a pencil in hand. The pencil wasn't meant for me, that I knew. Still, I would be granted opportunities to erase and try again. Reassured, I mustered up the courage to pick up my pen.

The message was simple but still a bit difficult to read. As I continued to write, I slowly got past the blur of dark paint that clouded my vision.

Losing my voice was a reminder to listen more than to speak. Old habits, not so easy to let go, needed to change. With eyes and ears finally open, life would be much easier to arrange.

Thinking back, the pencil was always resting securely in God's hand. Useless attempts to take back control had left it vulnerable, away from the safety of His grip. After so much struggle, the pencil was utterly crushed. Despite my own best efforts, the only thing to do was to trust.

My voice eventually returned, but silence was my newfound friend. While I wanted to speak my mind, I didn't feel the need to get my point across with force. Rather than raise my voice, I simply used my pen.

Though I was in the habit of grabbing pencils to rewrite and erase, I finally realized a need for change. Only God has the power to completely erase mistakes. Only by grace can the slate be wiped clean. I was writing freely with a pen in hand, and words flowed onto the page.

I turned to God and asked, "Why is there an eraser if I can only write with a pen?" He responded, "That is the eraser I have been using to purify your heart. I have had to erase and rewrite many of your stories to show that I was with you all along."

Thankfully, God never runs out of pencils. He offers freedom to try again and again. Pencil after pencil may grow dull, but a sharp pencil is hidden in every box. Laying beside that pencil is a brand new pen.

An ordered life was more about accepting what couldn't be controlled than trying to control it. It was more about being thankful for the progress made than wanting to go further. It was more about making the best of the cards given than wishing the deck had been dealt to me differently.

Orderliness wasn't always evident on the surface. It went far deeper than what the eye could see. In fact, I didn't need to have it all together. I needed to trust God with things that were out of my control, accept the unchangeable and just be me.

When I could accept uncontrollable, sometimes inevitable circumstances, balance was in reach. It wasn't an exact place or time. It was a state of thankful acceptance.

Pen in hand, I was on my way. I was able to speak again. But in many ways, my voice was still silenced. The value was in the journey, not when or how I would arrive.

Coming to terms with the concept of order, I realized that it genuinely was just an illusion. At times, balance led to a feeling of order. Other times, order resulted in some semblance of balance. But the burden was no longer mine to carry. And my art box sure felt lighter.

I set my pen down and placed it in the box. As I gently closed the lid, I noticed words of hope engraved on top. "Whether you turn to the right or to the left, your ears will hear a voice behind you, saying, 'This is the way; walk in it'"(Isaiah 30:21 NIV).

PROGRESS ISN'T JUST WHAT YOU DO TO MOVE FORWARD.
IT'S WHAT YOU LEAVE BEHIND TO KEEP MOVING.

WHAT FEELS LIKE A WRONG TURN
MIGHT BE JUST WHAT YOU NEED TO FIND YOUR WAY.

Julie Barbera

23 | Still in Time

"For the revelation awaits an appointed time;
it speaks of the end and will not prove false.
Though it linger, wait for it;
it will certainly come and will not delay."

(Habakkuk 2:3 NIV)

Was time chasing me or was I chasing time? Without approval, it freely went by. The beauty of the moment was lost if I lived in the past or focused too far ahead. Time was limited. It needed to be spent wisely. Perhaps slowing down would reveal its real value.

Two years had passed since I had started my writing journey. My family and I were on vacation in Villa de Leyva, Colombia. I hoped that I would find inspiration for the next chapter in my manuscript.

Mindful of the moment, time somehow stood still for me. Majestic mountains were in the distance. Fluffy clouds appeared within reach. The sun set on the horizon as dim twilight transitioned to dark night.

While I relished the scene, worries of the world quickly faded away. Speaking to the heart, the sublime view demanded excellence. My expectations were lifted. Feelings of insignificance no longer limited the greatness within me. Lost in time, I was inspired to reach far and wide. Everything seemed possible, if only for an instant. I mentally snapped a picture to trap the moment in my mind.

My eyes were fixed on timeless mountains that stretched to the clouds. It appeared as if they were high enough to touch heaven. They had stood tall for centuries, and I imagined that they had seen a lot. *What would they share if they could speak? Would they talk about things missed or misunderstood?*

Surrounded by Villa de Leyva's cobblestone streets, storybook houses and shops lined a busy courtyard. Locals blended into the scene. This made tourists easier to spot. Those living there seemed to be at ease, yet lost in an earlier time. Maybe we were the ones who were lost, always rushing through life.

Years had passed, and much had changed in my life since our last visit. But many aspects of the town remained the same. The picturesque scene seemed frozen in time. Although the story picked up where it left off, something felt distinctly different.

Leaning down to pick up a pebble, I noticed footprints. Moments passed by quickly. Collecting stones was a way to hold on to them. The trail started suddenly, and then mysteriously disappeared. Imprints left behind were a reminder that many others had walked the same path. Yet, I would never know where the road had taken them.

Pebbles, like memories, were cherished then quickly forgotten. The idea was that they would be remembered at a later time. I usually carried a bag to collect them. That day I accidentally left it behind, so I used my jacket pocket.

Walking along, my older son made an observation. He quietly asked, "Mommy, why do you have some gray hairs on your head?" My younger son overheard and quickly chimed in, "Yeah, I see them too, Mommy." I turned to my sons and smiled. It felt more appropriate to shrug off their remarks. Still, I was left to deal with reality. Time had gone by too fast to put into words.

We found a quaint restaurant in the main square and sat outside to enjoy the view. Plaza Mayor was brimming with life. Even so, time stood still. Every passerby had a story to tell, and no two stories were the same. Memories were imprinted on cobblestone streets. Every pebble had a purpose, and every footprint had a name.

Every passerby had a story to tell, and no two stories were the same. Memories were imprinted on cobblestone streets. Every pebble had a purpose, and every footprint had a name.

In deep thought, I was startled when a waitress came up from behind to take our order. Quick to make a selection, I was anxious to get back to the view. Everyone at the table, myself included, seemed lost in the moment.

Focused on vibrant activity, a group of stray dogs blended into the scene. Mostly unnoticed, they aimlessly roamed the streets. My sons noticed them right away and ran to the rescue. Pieces of food in hand, they darted into the center of the plaza.

In the distance, I saw a young woman. Her resemblance to me was striking: she looked like my double. She was pushing a baby stroller. A man and child were by her side.

The woman slowly approached our table. Up close, something seemed very familiar. Our eyes met for just an instant. Suddenly, I imagined myself in her shoes.

Close to a decade had passed since I had last walked these memorable streets. *Had I reached my goals? Had pebbles gathered helped or hindered my progress?*

That afternoon was distinctly different. There was something about Spanish cottages lining cobbled streets. Terra-cotta roofs and green trimmed houses welcomed all. Even the most transient of visitors felt at home in Villa de Leyva.

Rolling hills, mountains, and a serene, blue sky beckoned me to reach high. Years sped by with many wasted moments. Yet, the time had a way of speaking through silence.

Glimpses of mysterious beauty swiftly faded. Lost in the monotony of life, quickly forgotten, the only blessing was in the remembering. Years passed like droplets, dripping ever so slowly from a faucet. But the sink filled unnoticed and washed dreams away.

The food finally arrived, interrupting my daydream. I gestured for my sons to come back to the table. They returned, stray dogs close by. They sat down, but thoughts seemed to be with new friends waiting within sight. My younger son turned to my husband and asked, "Daddy, can we play with the dogs after we eat?" My husband responded with a smile.

Being outside gave us a fantastic view of the town. Still, some things could only be experienced hands on. We finished our meal, then all ventured into the streets.

The woman seemed to end up everywhere we went. We approached a poncho shop, and I saw her standing inside. She glanced across the room and looked me straight in the eye. Her family laughed and played as they tried on ponchos and hats. Yet, she looked disconnected. I quickly realized she wasn't staring at me. Instead, she was gazing at her reflection in the mirror.

Able to see through a sizable storefront window, I was on the outside looking in. Quickly losing track of time, I drifted into a daydream. When I awoke, my family had vanished. The young woman was gone as well.

Stepping away from the entrance, I made my way down a narrow side street. My focus shifted to coloring books propped up in a small storefront window. Still searching, there was no time for distraction. I glanced into the shop then scanned the perimeter. Stray dog friends were waiting outside. I quickly recognized them from the restaurant and stepped inside.

Familiar voices were coming from somewhere in the store. As I suspected, my family was there. The boys were sitting at a table nestled in the corner. Crayons, colored pencils and paper were spread across the table. Since I wanted to join them, I made a beeline to the window and grabbed a display coloring book.

The goal was to find a picture: a pebble. The idea was to hold on to memories and capture feelings from earlier in the day. As we carefully turned each page, detailed drawings left little room for original thought. Outlines were ready to be filled. Selecting color was the final, simple task.

Suddenly, the front door opened. Hearing familiar voices, I peeked around the corner. Again it was that woman: my double. She and her family were walking around the store. *Why was she everywhere I went?*

It was time to leave. The kids picked up their drawings, and we quietly left the store. The strays were missing when we walked outside. The moment we got to the door, my older son asked, "Mommy and Daddy, where did the dogs go?" I responded, "They must have left to play." I didn't want to show emotion, but I was also sad that they had gone their own way.

We passed Spanish cottages lining cobblestone streets. Each one was unique. They were like tiny models, only they were enlarged with bright color and intricate design. Porches covered with flowers created a picturesque scene.

Camera in hand, we had one last chance to gather pebbles. It was essential to capture memories before they were forgotten. My husband signaled for us to stand in front of a white cottage. Then he snapped several pictures to capture brief moments in time.

Leaning down to pick up a pebble, I glimpsed at my double out of the corner of my eye. She walked in the opposite direction then turned the corner. That was the last time I saw her, but her image lingered in my mind.

As we drove away from Plaza Mayor, cobbled streets faded into the distance. Reflections from the moon lit up the town. An outline of the mountain was visible under the nighttime sky.

You see, time somehow stood still that beautiful evening. Years mysteriously crossed. This made it possible to reflect on the past, yet be mindful of the present. But time wasn't frozen for long. It only stood still long enough for me to see.

With so much life to be lived, days were far too short to squander away. Pebbles became my memories. More aware of the moment, I resolved to gather more along the way.

Back on the main road en route to Bogota, the charming town turned into a distant memory. Visibility was significantly weakened by dense fog. A cloudy mist surrounded us on every side. We traveled up a narrow, winding road as memories of Villa de Leyva faded away.

Watching from the backseat, I was unable to make out a clear path ahead. Vivid images seemed far behind as I looked out the back window. Taking my eyes off the road for just an instant, I picked up my pebble bag and placed a handful of memories inside.

Returning to the city, fond recollections of the town were securely tucked away. Reflections hidden in my heart were tangible proof. I had also accumulated quite a few pebbles along the way.

Back from Villa de Leyva, we had a day left, so we decided to spend it with my husband's brother. We were waiting in his living room when he came out with a big surprise. He was holding an old cylinder container. My husband recognized it instantly, while I had no idea what was inside.

As a small child, my husband had saved every stamp and coin he could get his hands on. He didn't travel any further than Bogota, yet he had managed to build up quite an extensive collection. He had removed stamps from packages his father received, and he had held on to coins that others viewed as insignificant.

While his interests changed as a young adult, he still sensed that his collection had great value. He stored it in a compartment above his closet, securely tucked away and well-hidden. Little did he know, his brother was watching.

Years later, his mother needed to move, and they had to clear everything out of the house. His younger brother remembered the collection. To protect it, he removed it from the closet. Something prompted him not to say a word, and he secretly held on to it for years.

Why? The answer is unclear. What is clear is that he recognized its worth. The assortment was more valuable than money. The value was in the memories. It was no simple task for a young child to build up such a collection.

Our younger son, an avid coin and stamp collector, felt like he had found a treasure. While in Colombia, he was diligently searching for coins and stamps. Receiving this gift was a real blessing.

For whatever reason, my brother-in-law decided to share the collection with us that day. I suppose he had guarded it for such a time as this. At that moment, the past and the present became as one.

The coins and stamps were hidden gems to be unearthed at the right time. The timing never seemed quite right. Hence, they ended up in a dark closet for decades.

Lost treasures only benefit the person who finds them. Sadly, far too many are left behind. While the timing may not seem right, it's beneficial to pull them out of the closet from time to time.

Receiving this gift at just the right moment was a clear demonstration that our days are in God's hands. Only He knows the purpose. Only He sees the plan.

Sitting on the plane, we prepared for takeoff. Visions of Colombia were still fresh in mind. Pacing the runway, the wait felt like an eternity. All too often in a rush, memories of rolling hills and mountains prompted me to slow down.

Glancing down at a handful of memories, I opened my bag. Ever so carefully, I dropped a pebble and a silver coin inside. I hoped that I would get a final glimpse of reflections left behind. Then, I looked out the window one last time.

The plane accelerated quickly. Suddenly, all wheels were off the ground. When we were out of control in the air, God held us up with His hands. Securing pebbles from the past, present and future, our days were in the palm of His hands. I was uncertain of the future. Only God knew for sure. Flying high above the mountains, time truly stood still.

> When we were out of control in the air, God held us up with His hands. Securing pebbles from the past, present and future, our days were in the palm of His hands.

In the present time, I had come full circle in my quest. *Was I the pursuer or was I being pursued?* Although time is fleeting, it offers new opportunities every day. It's a precious gift that must be spent wisely. A choice is there to be made.

As I looked down to place another pebble in my bag, I heard a gentle whisper. "For I know the plans I have for you," declares the Lord, "plans to prosper you and not to harm you, plans to give you hope and a future" (Jeremiah 29:11 NIV).

———

**ENJOY THE JOURNEY AS YOU HEAD TO YOUR DESTINATION.
MAKE THE MOST OF TODAY.**

**LIVE IN THE MOMENT, VISION IN SIGHT.
KEEP YOUR FEET ON THE GROUND, YET REACH FOR THE SKY.**

———

Julie Barbera

24 | Good Enough

"Not that we are competent in ourselves
to claim anything for ourselves,
but our competence comes from God."

(2 Corinthians 3:5 NIV)

W as my glass half full or was it half empty? Seeing life
through two sets of lenses only seemed to cloud my view.
While there were moments when I saw through lenses of possibilities, I saw mostly limitations. Perhaps I needed to change my
perspective.

I sat in life's classroom a majority of the time. There was
always a lesson to learn. My name started with B, so I usually

ended up in front. While I thought that merely going to class was enough, I wondered if this was indeed the case.

Were challenges stopping me or was I stopping myself? My perception was everything. It ultimately determined the outcome. Even so, a familiar feeling of not being good enough always reared its ugly head. At the most inopportune times, it popped up. When I was about to take a step, it was there to stop me.

Was I good enough or not? A feeling of not measuring up greatly affected my perception. Yet, it was possible to change my perspective. Circumstances in life weren't really the culprit. They lost the power to influence my reality when I realized I could change my mindset.

Circumstances in life weren't really the culprit. They lost the power to influence my reality when I realized I could change my mindset.

Life was the ultimate classroom. I was a perpetual student. The truth was revealed in ways that could be understood. Creativity made it easier to accept. I struggled more than I would like to admit.

Lessons were broken down into weeks rather than days. Many needed to be repeated. Though some were hard to grasp, my teacher was patient. Grace made teachings easier to absorb. Some days were more difficult than others, and this was one I would have gladly missed.

In life's classroom, you need to show up daily. There is no room for skipping. One missed teaching affects the next. Good and bad, every lesson has value. There is a reason for every experience.

Learning to view life with optimism was a familiar subject. It was taught many times before, but each time the presentation was a little different. As simple as it seemed, this lesson was one that required constant reteaching. While the truth wasn't always easy to see, it would be revealed in time.

When I walked into a classroom, glasses lined a table in front. Some were full, and others were empty. Most were degrees of half-full and half-empty. Perplexed, I wondered what I was missing.

The glasses were separated into categories. When I looked closely, labels provided a clue. Challenges and limitations made up one. Potential and possibilities made up another. Others couldn't be categorized.

There was quite a difference between glasses in each group. Some were tall and narrow. Water filled them, but it was below the fifty percent mark. This made them look emptier. Others were short and wide. More than fifty percent full, they looked even fuller.

Pebbles were stacked up at the end of the table. Varying in size and shape, each affected the water differently. Larger stones had a tendency to push the water to the top. At times, this caused it to overflow. Smaller rocks made little impact. The only effect was a slight splash or movement.

Pebbles were there for a reason: to show how experiences cleared or clouded the view. Everyone's perception was different. What caused a small ripple for one created an overflow for another.

Life's experiences were like pebbles. Some were positive, and others were negative. In many ways, situations affected me more than most. Every little rock dropped into my half-empty glass caused it to overflow.

A negative mindset made it hard to be optimistic. Even if positivity was looking me straight in the eye, my focus shifted to what could go wrong. At times circumstances seemed right, but I still found something to worry me. It felt more comfortable to prepare for the worst since something could go wrong.

Like every good student, I showed up for class. I must admit,

I was tired of going. I felt that merely showing up would take me closer to the goal. In a way, I was right. Essential lessons needed to be learned, and I had to at least do my part.

The class was ready to begin; it was time to take a seat. Since it was a repeat lesson, the room was packed. The teacher waited patiently as students shuffled around in search of a chair.

Blocking out noise, I shifted my focus to the tall glasses lined up in front. I was sitting in the front row. I would have had a perfect view, but the tall glasses made it hard to see beyond the first row.

The students were finally seated. The teacher asked for volunteers. They were to write down the furthest row of glasses clearly visible from their seat. I looked back. The class was seven rows deep. One from each row was to come forward to write a number on the board. I volunteered for the first row.

Since I was seated in front, my view was blocked. Lined up like soldiers, challenges and limitations stood tall. Surprisingly, I was only able to make out the first row. It seemed unreasonable that anyone would see beyond it.

I tended to look at the world through clouded lenses. I often wondered how people were able to turn negative into positive. Some had significant challenges, yet they seemed to overcome them with ease. I had my own set of problems, but I made them more significant than what they really needed to be.

Perception was different for all. Distance affected sight much less than anticipated. Being in the back didn't mean the view would be blocked. Sitting in front didn't guarantee a clear view.

Some seated all the way in the back were able to see past six rows. They saw even the smallest of possibilities lining the back row. Others, seated in front, were unable to look past the front row. They couldn't see beyond the glasses towering over even the greatest of possibilities.

My attention shifted to a large board hanging on the door.

Written in black marker, with letters large enough to see from any angle in the room, the agenda read:

Lesson 1: Looking past half-empty glasses makes half-full glasses easier to see.

Lesson 2: Everyone has challenges and limitations. Accept them, whatever they might be.

Lesson 3: Learn to count possibilities rather than limitations. This always makes it easier to see.

Lesson 4: Life is short. Make the most of potential and opportunity.

The real challenge seemed to be getting past a feeling of not being good enough. I pondered the idea. *Is anyone ever truly good enough?* Maybe it wasn't my position in the room that blocked the view. Perhaps it was something else.

Suddenly, I visualized myself walking up to the table. I stared down at the challenges and limitations. Towering above potential and possibilities, I finally saw them for what they were. They were intimidating from my seat. Leaving no space in between, insecurity and doubt stood tall like guards. They blocked my ability to see, and their identities were clear. While it wasn't always possible to eliminate them, I needed to accept and look past them.

The class was finally over. Students were much quieter leaving than when they arrived. As I made my way to the door, confidence built up inside. I looked down at the glasses lined up side by side. Up close, challenges and limitations didn't seem as threatening. Able to see possibilities, there were far more than expected.

An overview of this week's teaching was on the front table. I stopped to pick up my homework to be completed in between lessons. An inspiring message was written on the board to serve as a reminder.

Everyone struggles with something. The key is learning to accept it whatever it might be. Learn to count blessings rather than limitations. This always makes it easier to see.

When I came back for the second lesson, I noticed a change in my thinking. Time to reflect seemed to alter my view. As we had done the week prior, students were asked to write down the furthest row of glasses clearly visible from their seats. Once again, I volunteered for the front row.

Everyone struggles with something. The key is learning to accept it whatever it might be. Learn to count blessings rather than limitations. This always makes it easier to see.

This time, I was able to see past the first row. Potential and possibilities seemed within reach. The tall glasses were no longer intimidating. The half-empty glasses even looked a little fuller this week.

The tall glasses were still lined up in front, but they didn't completely block my view. I was able to see them for what they were. No longer seen as insurmountable obstacles, they had no more power than I was willing to give them.

Blocking possibilities, challenges and limitations still stood tall like soldiers prepared for battle. Towering over potential, narrow-mindedness obstructed my view. Open-mindedness was key. I learned to look past half-empty glasses, and this made half-full glasses easier to see.

As a perpetual student in life's classroom, I would need the same lesson time and again. This wasn't my first class, nor would it be my last. But for the first time, I was willing to accept the outcome either way.

Writing the challenges on paper somehow made them look smaller that day. Even those previously viewed as limitations weren't really disadvantages at all. They were simply pebbles gathered along the way.

Leaving more confident than I had arrived, I glanced back at the glasses lined with hope. Now that I was finally able to see past the first two rows, limitations guarded possibilities with all their might. Although they were still there, something was different. They were seen as advantages: opportunities to learn lessons in life.

When I focused on the half-full glasses, dreams felt within reach. I wanted to finish my manuscript. I was determined to follow my heart. And doubt no longer had the power to stop me.

Coming to terms with *good enough* had more to do with accepting myself. It wasn't about meeting a set of standards. All fall short. Everyone has room for improvement.

Shortfalls no longer defined me. The pain turned into my passion. Challenges made me a champion, and the struggle became my story. I found the courage to take a chance.

While the glasses still looked half empty at times, this was normal and something I needed to accept. But having learned to see life through positive lenses, negativity lost its grip. With God as my teacher, and the Bible as a guide, the half-full glasses slowly became more visible over time.

When I opened the door to leave, words of hope were posted outside the classroom. The message read: "My grace is sufficient for you, for my power is made perfect in weakness" (2 Corinthians 12:9 NIV).

———————

**BEING POSITIVE DOESN'T MEAN THINGS WILL GO YOUR WAY.
YOU'LL FIND THE POSITIVE NO MATTER HOW THINGS GO.**

**DWELL ON WHAT CAN GO WRONG, AND YOU'LL FEAR EVERYTHING.
FOCUS ON ALL THAT CAN GO RIGHT,
AND YOU'LL FIND THE COURAGE TO DO ANYTHING.**

———————

Julie Barbera

25 | Unhidden Potential

"Having then gifts differing according to the grace
that is given to us, *let us use them.*"

(Romans 12:6 NKJV)

W as the gift hidden or had it already been revealed? Either
way, I searched for pearls. I picked up shells along the
shore. They were naturally brought in by the tide. While they
were right before my eyes, I still wondered if there was a treasure
at the bottom of the sea.

Potential stretched as far as the ocean was wide. Even so, I
tended to dwell on limitations. I was aware of all the probabili-
ties, but I focused on what could go wrong rather than all that
could go right.

This was another one of life's lessons. Nature was the class-room, and a beach chair was my seat. Grains of sand were like endless possibilities. The vast, open sea made way for limitless opportunities. Each shell was a hidden treasure. *But was there really a message for me?*

It was a cool, windy day. Sand beat against everything in its path. Notebook in hand, I sat on the beach alone. I stayed behind to work on my manuscript. Meanwhile, my family searched for seashells in the distance.

Inspiration was hard to find, but I couldn't force it. That made moments like these invaluable. Each chapter came in God's timing, and ideas blew by like a breeze. I had a choice: capture them in writing or let them drift away with the wind.

My book was the treasure. Words from God were secret gems. The lessons came with the moment. I didn't want to miss them as some disregard shells in the sand. If I failed to capture a moment, I just might overlook a hidden gem.

I have lived close to the ocean for roughly twenty years. In the past ten years, I can literally count the number of times I have gone to the beach on both hands. I suppose I have taken it for granted.

Frankly, I don't like sand. It's messy and covers everything in its path. Any pleasure associated with a sunny day at the shore is quickly washed away by the mess. This makes going a nuisance, so I try to avoid it.

My kids recently convinced me to spend the afternoon at the beach. I was hesitant, but they were insistent. Sadly, my feelings were justified when we ended up with a car full of sand. The sand that started in our car made it to our house. An afternoon that was supposed to be relaxing turned into nothing more than work.

The boys enjoyed building sand castles and wanted to go back the following week. I needed time to recover from the previous week's mess. Despite my hesitation, they talked me into it again.

Truthfully speaking, I was focused on the negative aspects of going to the beach. I failed to see the positive. In reality, there was far more positive than negative. I minimized the beauty and magnified the mess. I somehow missed relaxing waves, sparkling sand and the calm, blue sky. They were nothing more than background scenery.

Grains of sand lined the shore. Each one looked the same. They were so small, and it was impossible to count them all. Alone, they seemed to lack importance; they merely blended into the scene. Together they were significant: part of something greater than themselves.

The ocean stretched far and wide. I felt like a tiny speck compared to the vast, open sea. A sense of insignificance made the truth hard to see. I tended to overlook the potential inside. I failed to recognize the opportunities right in front of me.

A handful of gifts were concealed like a hidden treasure. These were the pearls. Only a couple were scattered along the shore. Like dreams, it took courage to believe. Yet, I was determined to find them all.

Many gifts had already been revealed, and these were the gems. They were just below the sand's surface. Like shells brought in by the tide, these talents came naturally to me. But I tended to overlook them.

While the beauty of simplicity was all around, I made things far more complicated than they needed to be. I was always searching for something more. Beautiful things in life are simple. At times, they are so simple that we miss them. Gems were already in my hands, yet I continued to search for pearls at the bottom of the sea.

I somehow saw myself in sparkling grains of sand: insignificant yet significant at the same time. I wanted to stand out, yet I held potential in. I wanted to be accepted, only I didn't accept myself. I tried to fit in with the group, but I didn't think like the group.

Life had to have a deeper meaning. I would never be satisfied with just fitting in. I was determined to find a purpose. There had to be more. I tried so hard to fit in that I failed to stand out. Perhaps I wasn't meant to fit in. Maybe I was supposed to stand out. If I wanted to stand out, I needed the courage to step out.

The risk was great. There was a chance I would make a mistake. Maybe it was best to stay in my place. While it felt safer, I still held on to hope that my one day would eventually come.

I wasn't looking for a message that day. Inspiration somehow found me. That was the way it worked. At the most unexpected of times, God showed up with a word.

I had hit a bump in the road with my manuscript. I had reached a point in my journey where I couldn't just sit back and write. It was time to turn the page. The next chapter was waiting for me, only this time, something was different.

The ocean seemed to be calling me out of complacency. My potential would never be revealed from a beach chair. Possibilities would never be realized if I stood still.

Up to this point, inspiration had come from experience. God had given me ideas. I had simply waited for insight. Content had come quickly, and words had flowed naturally. It was as if I had watched a movie on the big screen.

It was time to make my own movie. I couldn't sit back and passively watch the same film. I needed to step out. I had to trust that God would be there to meet me. This was the hardest part of my journey.

The ocean seemed to be calling me out of complacency. My

potential would never be revealed from a beach chair. Possibilities would never be realized if I stood still.

While I had my doubts, I was waiting to be sure. Perhaps I would never be 100 percent certain. Suddenly, a simple, yet profound thought came to mind. *I would rather doubt myself moving forward than wait to be sure standing still.*

This message did more than speak to my heart; it changed my heart. Taking a chance was something I had talked about for years. I had dreamed about it more nights than I had slept. I had visualized it more times than I had looked at my reflection in the mirror.

Dreams don't sleep. A vision doesn't rely on a mirror. Dreams live in the heart. We rest, but they remain restless. A vision doesn't depend on anything for its reflection. Every vision has a light. That light shines brightly, even in the darkest of hours. It stays on, and nothing can put it out.

At times, it's necessary to look inside. Truth is visible with or without a mirror. Reflections are clear, even through the cracks. Potential isn't something to find. It's already inside. Possibilities aren't just in dreams. It takes faith to believe.

I somehow found the faith to take a chance. I finally mustered up the courage to walk toward my mountain. I was at the doors of social media. I was literally behind the curtain ready to walk toward the podium. My manuscript wasn't just an idea. It was a book.

With my speech in hand, I anxiously approached the podium. Books were stacked up on a table outside the auditorium. I would sign copies after my presentation.

The microphone was set up and ready to go. The room was full of people. I was nervous yet unafraid. *Was this just a dream? Or, was I about to step into my destiny?*

Perhaps there was a treasure at the bottom of the sea, but I would never find it if I missed shells lining the shore. I needed every gem to search the depths of the sea. One day I would find hidden pearls. This is how I would become who God had called me to be.

As I turned to leave, my son ran up to me with a bucketful of seashells. Ready to dump the treasures in the sand, I hesitated for a moment. Seashells don't really talk, but they spoke to my heart that day.

The microphone was set up and ready to go. The room was full of people. I was nervous yet unafraid. *Was this just a dream? Or, was I about to step into my destiny?*

"You are the light of the world. A town built on a hill cannot be hidden. Neither do people light a lamp and put it under a bowl. Instead they put it on its stand, and it gives light to everyone in the house. In the same way, let your light shine before others, that they may see your good deeds and glorify your Father in heaven" (Matthew 5:14-16 NIV).

————

TREASURES ARE RIGHT BEFORE OUR EYES, YET MANY MISS GEMS
SEARCHING FOR PEARLS AT THE BOTTOM OF THE SEA.

POTENTIAL ISN'T SOMETHING TO FIND. IT'S ALREADY INSIDE.
POSSIBILITIES AREN'T JUST IN DREAMS. IT TAKES FAITH TO BELIEVE.

————

Julie Barbera

26 | A Reflection Made Clear

"For now we see only a reflection as in a mirror;
then we shall see face to face. Now I know in part;
then I shall know fully, even as I am fully known."

(1 Corinthians 13:12 NIV)

W as my reflection clear or was I unable to see beyond the cracks? Either way, I had to look in the mirror. I wasn't sure if what I saw reflected the truth. And I wondered how I ever saw clearly. Perhaps light can still shine brightly, even through the cracks.

This was another lesson in life's classroom. It was harder than most. Unlike many others, it needed to be experienced. While I could wait for inspiration to move me, I couldn't move to the next chapter without action. I needed to be willing to step outside of my comfort zone.

The same movie had played in my mind for years. I had watched it on the big screen again and again. With the TV stuck on the same channel, I had a remote control in hand and kept rewinding back to my favorite parts. The days of passive contemplation were over. Inspiration was still there, but I had to look a little harder to find it.

I remember the day I started my manuscript. I recall the hour I found the courage to take a chance. I think back on the moment I took a step toward my mountain. Although I lived out these moments in my mind, I was unable to act on them. Taking action was by far the hardest part.

The moments of decision were easy yet hard at the same time. They required courage, but they gave me strength. Hope was alive. Dreams felt possible. Even so, complacency quickly set in.

Contentment was deceiving. It had a way of sneaking up on me when I least expected it. It had a way of making me accept it. It comforted me with the idea that my one day would eventually come. At the same time, it planted seeds of reasonable doubt.

I went right back to talking about what I would do. I dreamed about how I would do it. I visualized what it would be like. My vision went back to being nothing more than just a dream.

For years, I talked about standing on the mountain. I was on stage, and I had written many books. I was speaking in front of thousands in many languages. I was helping people around the world.

While I appeared strong on the outside, that didn't necessarily reflect what was going on inside. Others didn't know that I was full of doubt. I shared the vision to keep it alive. I wanted to believe in my heart, and my greatest fear was being wrong.

The timing was never right. Circumstances were never ideal. I was never good enough, and nothing was up to my standards.

Life had a way of revealing cracks. Although I had many, they had nothing to do with weaknesses. I was simply unable to accept imperfections. This was my most significant shortcoming.

In reality, everyone has flaws. I saw mine clearly. Others weren't really paying attention to my imperfections like I thought. I realize that now. They were too focused on their own, yet the fear of what they might say stopped me.

God used my manuscript to teach many lessons. It took twenty-five chapters to learn that I needed to accept cracks. This was the greatest lesson of all.

After five years of reflection, I had come full circle. A published book wasn't my destination. While it was an essential part of the journey, it was just the beginning. Writing helped me to move forward, and I needed strength for the road ahead.

A launched website didn't mean others would read my content. A social media presence didn't guarantee that I would be liked. Hours spent on podcast messages didn't mean others would listen. Heartfelt blog messages posted on social media wouldn't always get likes.

Responses from others didn't make me worthy. I was worthy because God said I was worthy. This was my calling, and nothing could stop me. I didn't have to prove this to others. I needed to convince myself. It was then and only then that I would find the courage to take a chance.

The competition was fierce out there since many others were doing the same. It was going to be hard to stand out. This became evident the moment I stepped out. I needed courage, more than I ever thought. The road ahead was long, longer than I ever imagined. I felt weak, but I was stronger than expected.

Over time, the message became even more apparent. I was meant to be a leader, not a follower. Still, I had a lot to learn. Leaders would come in time. I needed to know which to follow and which to ignore. Perhaps there was something to learn from all of them.

It was possible to stand out, but I needed to find my way. Social media followers would come and go. Many followed to be followed back, while some came in just to get a click. I couldn't take it personally. It was no reflection of me. My strength needed to go beyond what the eye could see.

It was easier to change just to fit in. It was harder to keep it real, yet this is how I would stand out.

Everything looked easy until I stepped into it. Doing it was the hard part. My messaging needed to be clear. More importantly, I needed to stay real.

It was time to create my own movie. God was the director and producer, and I was the leading actress. I needed to step onto the set. I needed to play my part. I couldn't play anyone else's role but my own. This was a clear reflection.

If I stepped out to deliver a message, the hardest part was authenticity. I needed to stay true to who I was and why I started. It was easier to change just to fit in. It was harder to keep it real, yet this is how I would stand out.

Purpose challenged me to question what I had been taught. Focus forced me to think beyond what I could see. Destiny prompted me to look past the facade.

Purpose isn't about perfection. Destiny isn't about dreams, and focus isn't about fantasy. Purpose is about the plan. Destiny requires determination, and focus relies on faith.

God had a plan, and I was determined. But the plan would only come to fruition with unwavering determination. This was an accurate reflection in the mirror.

A mirror is simple. It reflects an image. Yet, how I viewed that image changed my reality. What I saw had the power to make or break me. Doubt saw flaws and weaknesses. Hope saw blessings and strengths. A simple reflection changed everything.

A mirror reflects what's outside. Words echo what's in the heart. Light can shine brightly, even through the cracks. Change starts inside then reflects outside. If transformed inside, outside influences lose power. Then, it's possible to make an impact.

A vision doesn't rely on a mirror. It reflects its own light. Its light is always on, and nothing can put it out. My reflection needed to match my vision. I needed to visualize myself doing it, then I would.

A mirror is simple.
It reflects an image.
Yet, how I viewed
that image changed
my reality.

Although I still had my doubts, I was able to see past them. My role was linked to purpose. There was a why behind why I started, and I could never lose sight of that. At last, I found the courage to look at myself in the mirror.

My reflection was different than what I imagined. In many ways, it was easier to accept. In some ways, it was harder. Either way, a clear reflection made the truth easier to see.

God had undoubtedly prepared me for such a time as this. I had what was required for the journey, but I needed strength to stay the course. It was by enduring trials that I would find purpose. I had a long way to go. Regardless, I found courage beyond the cracks.

As I stepped away from the mirror, I looked down at my cell phone. God didn't need a mobile device to spread the word, but it was a tool. It was merely a way to get the word out. There was a world out there that needed a positive message, and I had a role to play. I heard a beep, and then a text popped up on my screen. "Commit to the Lord whatever you do, and he will establish your plans" (Proverbs 16:3 NIV).

PURPOSE KEEPS YOU GOING WHEN ALL ELSE TELLS YOU TO QUIT.
STAY FOCUSED ON WHY YOU STARTED.

DON'T DWELL ON WHAT YOU DON'T HAVE, HOW YOU FALL SHORT.
FOCUS ON WHAT YOU HAVE TO GIVE, WHAT MAKES YOU STAND OUT.

Julie Barbera

27 | Expectations Revealed

"There is surely a future hope for you,
and your hope will not be cut off."

(Proverbs 23:18 NIV)

Did I expect things to go as planned or was I prepared for the unexpected? Either way, I was moving forward. Although I had come a long way, I had a long trip ahead of me. I needed courage for the journey, and this was just the beginning.

My action demonstrated faith, yet inaction was my greatest challenge. Expectations had already been revealed. They were made known, one by one. Some of God's expectations for me were optimistic, yet uncomfortable. Others felt unrealistic, yet possible. And for the very first time in my life, I was grounded in my vision.

Wisdom led to insight. Knowledge was power, and there was always something new to learn. Every lesson was a part of the plan, and I needed to go back to the classroom once again. While lessons came unexpectedly, all arrived at just the right time.

It was Independence Day, 2017. I looked up at the nighttime sky. The beach was crowded. Family by my side, we waited for the fireworks show to begin. While there in presence, my mind drifted to another place in time. I had just started a new section in my manuscript. And like every chapter, it forced me to turn the page.

My vision hadn't quite turned out as planned. In reality, I was waiting for fireworks. I thought the story would end with me on stage. I would be liked and admired. My content would be valued. This was how I envisioned the final chapter.

It took courage to believe in my hopes and dreams. Hope kept the vision alive. While vision brought truth to light, life was full of responsibility. Reality had a way of setting in. My biggest challenge was balancing daily life with dreams.

Although I was sure the vision would one day come to pass, the end was just the beginning. The message in my manuscript wasn't about doing. It was about building the courage to act.

After years of writing, I had come full circle. I had to interpret what I had written. I needed to relive chapters to rewrite them, and the thought overwhelmed me.

The fireworks show wasn't as spectacular as anticipated. It never seemed to meet my expectations. The grand finale felt like the beginning, and then it quickly came to an end.

Although the show fell short, it spoke to my heart. The message was about expectations. Life was full of them. While I had big plans for the future, things wouldn't always go as planned. In short, I needed to be prepared for the unexpected.

My family and I left the beach and made our way down

Atlantic Blvd. The street was crowded on both sides. Thousands had come out to celebrate, yet very few looked excited.

The crowd was behind me. This prompted me to walk faster, but it didn't overwhelm me. A flood of people marched toward me. Going against the masses was tough, yet I walked with my head held high.

The next stage of my journey came with many unknowns. My faith still wavered at times, and my family wasn't very supportive of my vision. While I felt alone in my walk, I resolved to remain faithful to what God had called me to do.

The challenge was in remaining true to my message. It was vital to stay the course, even if others pushed against me. Confidence would help me to stand tall, even when shoved to the side.

Walking toward the crowd was a reminder that I needed to go against the group at times. This was how I would eventually help those in the crowd. Many wouldn't agree with my vision or message. Regardless, I needed to be strong. This would allow me to stand for something greater than myself.

A drawbridge was up ahead. It was lifted to allow large boats to pass. Everyone waited for a signal to cross. The bridge came down, and hundreds began to move at once.

As we approached the bridge, I was concerned. The crowd was massive. I wondered if the bridge could hold the weight. Walking hand in hand with my son, we looked down. Metal holes made it possible to see the water below. My son turned to me and asked, "Mommy, what if the bridge collapses?" Ironically, the very same thought had just gone through my mind.

One foot in front of the other, we walked forward. I thought to myself, *Every step is a step of faith.* I was silent as we crossed. When I was almost at the end of the bridge, I made a connection. I turned to my son and stated, "We just have to walk by faith."

At that moment, a new story was created in my mind. I will admit, it wasn't a perfect story. It was full of twists and turns.

Setbacks came, and there were challenges along the way. What-ever the outcome, it was my story. I was ready for the next chapter. Every step was a step of faith.

There is a point in every journey where there is no turning back. I was at that point. I had gone too far to give up. It was time for the next phase. After a long wait, I was ready to open the curtain and step on stage.

I would soon send my book to the publisher, and that would start a new adventure. My vision was big. That part didn't change. What changed were my expectations. I had many, yet I was more grounded in reality. And for the very first time, I wasn't afraid.

I imagined myself on stage in front of thousands. My books were bestsellers, and I was a well-known speaker. I was out in the world making a difference.

My vision was perfectly clear. For years, I envisioned how the story would play out. There was no room for another dream. While I was on my way, my perception had changed. And I had somehow made space for a smaller vision.

> There is a point in every journey where there is no turning back. I was at that point. I had gone too far to give up.

I had walked the streets of Delray Beach on July 4th, 2017. A year had gone by, and I had come full circle. It was now July 4th, 2018. Although it took a year to see, expectations had been revealed. My clearest reflection of all was that I needed to be prepared for the unexpected.

A year prior, clear expectations were in mind. I was ready to submit my manuscript. I thought it would be published in a couple of months. In reality, it took almost two years.

My husband was perfectly healthy when we had walked the streets in 2017. At that time, he had resisted the vision. A year later, he was fully onboard. Shortly after the fireworks show, his health took a turn for the worse. Unexpected health challenges brought us closer together as a family. We were overwhelmed, but faith and vision kept us going.

While I still wanted to get to my destination, I was no longer concerned with how quickly I would arrive. After all, I was in pursuit of purpose. I never would have imagined that my circumstances would change so drastically in a year. Even so, God had prepared me for such a time as this. I had to remain faithful in the small things. The plan would unfold in time.

Even though I expected things to go as planned, I was prepared for the unexpected. The road ahead was longer than I ever imagined. I was determined to stay the course. I was ready to handle whatever life brought my way. And this was just the beginning.

For our nation, July 4th is a time of celebration. The focus is on liberty and our nation's independence. I was a part of this great nation my entire life. I lived in the land of the free, yet I lived in bondage. I was free but limited by my own beliefs.

I was a part of this great nation my entire life. I lived in the land of the free, yet I lived in bondage. I was free but limited by my own beliefs.

Independence meant so much more to me that day. It was about freedom from a feeling of not being good enough, fear of what others think, and a need to be perfect to start new projects. I had found the confidence to do what I love, love what I do and live with purpose. And most of all, I had built up the courage to become who God had called me to be.

When God's expectations were revealed, the vision was no

longer about me. It was about us. God had brought us closer as a family for such a time as this. And we were all stronger together.

The fireworks show was over, and my family and I were in the car. While I was there in presence, I was busy creating the final chapter. As I looked in the mirror, I noticed tiny cracks. Surprisingly, they didn't block my view as they did before. I saw clearly, even through them. And it was through these cracks in the mirror that all became clear.

Suddenly, my attention shifted to the fireworks in the distance. I looked out the window and saw words of hope written in the sky. "For I know the plans I have for you," declares the Lord, "plans to prosper you and not to harm you, plans to give you hope and a future" (Jeremiah 29:11 NIV).

IF YOU SET OUT TO MAKE A DIFFERENCE,
YOU MAY ENCOUNTER RESISTANCE.
DON'T AVOID IT. EMBRACE IT. BE THE DIFFERENCE.

MAKE A WAY WHERE THERE SEEMS TO BE NO WAY.
DON'T GO DOWN A BEATEN PATH.
PURSUE PURPOSE. PAVE YOUR OWN PATH.

Julie Barbera

Closing Words

"My grace is sufficient for you,
for my power is made perfect in weakness."

(2 Corinthians 12:9 NIV)

Thank you for joining me on this journey from fear and doubt to discover your courage. Remember, you already have what you need to fulfill your potential. Take both weaknesses and strengths, and use them to make a difference. There is no better moment than the present, and life has prepared you for such a time as this.

Perhaps you are saying to yourself: *But I have cracks.* And my response to you is "Yes, you do. And, so do I. Yet, it's through these cracks in the mirror that all becomes clear."

Perfection is just an illusion. Everyone has flaws. Even the tiniest lump of clay can be transformed into a treasured masterpiece. Circumstances don't define you. They shape you. Molded to make a difference, you can walk forward in God's grace.

Say goodbye to a need to be perfect to start. Release the fear of what others think. Move beyond a feeling of not being good enough. Build the courage to step outside your comfort zone. Do what you love, love what you do and live with purpose. And, most of all, become who God has called you to be. Let your light shine brightly, even through the cracks.

Many blessings,

Julie Barbera

The Journey Ahead

"Trust in the Lord with all your heart
and lean not on your own understanding;
in all your ways submit to him,
and he will make your paths straight."

(Proverbs 3:5-6 NIV)

Move Your Mountain

I t's time for a change, and you are sitting in front of your mountain with determination to make this a groundbreaking season in your life. But how do you find your breakthrough to genuinely break ground?

Perhaps you are like me, and you have been staring at the same mountain for years. You have finally built up the courage to walk toward your mountain, only it doesn't seem that it will move. You understand that you need to move big rocks out of the way. Yet, it appears that you will never make enough progress to leave a dent.

Maybe you have gone around the same mountain for longer than you can remember. At times, you pick up small pebbles. Other times, you build up the strength to move a rock or two. You are motivated for a while. It seems that you will break through to solid ground. You start then stop, but nothing happens. And it may be at the point that you are tempted to give up.

If you ever hope to break through to your potential, you need to step outside of your comfort zone. It isn't comfortable to move heavy rocks. It isn't easy to pick them up day after day. And the more stones you shift, the higher the probability of a landslide.

Each time you move a rock, there is a chance that others will fall. Despite the risk, you have to be willing to take a chance. At times, you may feel a need to make progress that you can see.

This will prompt you to move many rocks at once. Other times, it's best to be methodical. After all, consistency is key.

If you have a crane, this will allow you to move massive rocks out of the way. In turn, you will see fast, visible results. But if you are like me, resources are limited. You have to work with what you have, and what you have isn't equipped to move massive rocks all at once.

If you pick up one rock a day, it may feel like the mountain will never move. But if you are careful and consistent, you will leave time and space for the dust to settle. Other rocks will be affected by the change. The thoughtful movement will allow everything to fall into place. This will give you the balance to pick up rocks day after day.

CONSISTENCY IS KEY. PICK UP ONE ROCK A DAY.
ONE DAY YOU WILL LOOK BACK AND
REALIZE YOU MOVED A MOUNTAIN.

Julie Barbera

A Chance to Fly

While writing *Cracked Mirror, Clear Reflection,* I had an inspiring conversation with my thirteen-year-old son. I was a bit frustrated by a lack of progress. Although I was moving forward steadily, results hadn't come as quickly as expected. His wisdom and insight helped to change my perspective.

Sebastian said, "Mommy, it may feel like you are going around the runway forever, but you are on your way. Some are still sitting in the airport waiting to board. Others haven't even started the trip. While the wait may be longer than expected, you will eventually make it off the ground."

Pursuing dreams is like a plane trip. To start, you have to go to the airport. Your destination is clear, and you have a flight to catch. Hesitation sets in as you drive into the terminal parking lot. You have already canceled this flight several times before. The thought of being out of control in the air makes you feel uneasy. This time you make it to the airport, but the temptation to turn back hits you just before you board.

When you are finally on board, it feels like you are pacing the runway for an eternity. The delay is very frustrating since you have places to go and people to see. You remind yourself that the plane has to go through security checks. Preparation is required to ensure a smooth flight.

Air traffic controllers inform the pilot that it's time for takeoff.

Thankfully, they will be around to give instructions along the way.

Slowly but surely, the plane begins to lift off. Suddenly, you wish you were back in the terminal. Although it was frustrating to wait, you felt safe on the ground.

The flight doesn't start out as smooth as expected. This makes you wonder why you even boarded the plane. You calm down and remind yourself of all the preparation that led up to this day.

Although you experience sharp turns and turbulence, you are thankful that you are on your way. Ups and downs are a part of the flight. Others are still sitting in the airport waiting to board. While you may not have arrived, your destination is in sight. You simply need to trust by faith and hold on tightly.

The perfect moment will never arrive. Sometimes you need to take a chance, risk it all for a chance to fly.

"FOR ONCE YOU HAVE TASTED FLIGHT,
YOU WILL FOREVER WALK THE EARTH WITH YOUR
EYES TURNED SKYWARD, FOR THERE YOU HAVE BEEN,
AND THERE YOU WILL ALWAYS LONG TO RETURN."
-LEONARDO DA VINCI   *Julie Barbera*

When Opportunity Knocks

L ast night, I had a dream that Opportunity knocked on my door. In my dream, I was too blind to see. I frantically rushed to the door while taking care of my chores as the thought *no more* came to me.

In a panic, I opened the door and saw Opportunity staring me right in the face. With a smile I will never forget, he looked me straight in the eye. Then he said, "My dear friend, why don't you stop this race?"

I responded in a rush. "Not now. I have no time free. Time is something I lack right now, and I have no time to just be. I will tell you what, I would really love to step out after I have done all that I have to do. One thing is for sure. You can count on my word. When I am done, I will be sure to walk with you."

He softly smiled and then spoke in a calm voice, "I truly understand. You are busy right now. Go back to what you need to do."

A year had gone by. I was awake this time. Once again, I heard a knock at my door. Rushing around while taking care of my chores, I finished a project and then I stopped to mop the floor.

I frantically rushed to see who was there. I was greeted by Opportunity and Faith at my door. I was pleasantly surprised that Opportunity brought a friend this time. He hadn't forgotten about me for sure.

I spent a few moments and thanked them for their time. Then I said, "I really have to flee. I have so much to do. I truly appreciate the thought, but I only have a little time free."

Opportunity and Faith seemed to understand. They looked me in the eyes and said, "We would love to step out, but we will come back another day. We truly understand. It's no problem at all. Go back to what you need to do. When you have a few moments to spend with us, we will be right here waiting for you."

My friends, Opportunity and Faith, never seemed to forget. They dropped by time and time again. It seemed that I was always so busy rushing around. I never had a moment to spend with my faithful friends.

Years had gone by, and I was alone in my room. Once again, there was a knock at my door. Busier than ever, I laid my laptop down and picked up my keys. I was ready to run out to the store. I was overwhelmed with work without a moment to breathe. I called out, "Who is standing at the door?"

I heard a familiar voice, one I will never forget. I looked up to find Opportunity and Faith waiting at my door. Time was standing beside them, and I knew what this meant for me. My time had come. It was my turn to step out. I stood there alone while Time stared at me.

I remembered all the times that Opportunity and Faith had knocked on my door. I had been too blind to see. I had somehow thought that Opportunity would come back again, that he would bring me the faith to see. I realized that my life was passing me by. Now Time was there waiting for me.

If I could go back and live my life once again, I would be sure to live it differently. I would open the door to let Opportunity inside. I would allow Faith to live alongside me.

Time was standing there. I was given another chance. But I have something important to say. Don't take time for granted. Keep faith in your heart. Always be thankful for the day.

When Opportunity knocks, let him inside. Don't tell him to

come back another day. Above all else, one thing you should never forget: if asked to step out, never, ever push Opportunity away.

God had opened my eyes when He stood there with Time with His arms spread wide waiting for me. He clearly spoke these words in a voice I will never forget. "For I know the plans I have for you," declares the Lord, "plans to prosper you and not to harm you, plans to give you hope and a future." (Jeremiah 29:11 NIV).

A DREAM IS SIMPLY A DREAM UNTIL YOU ACT.
HAVE A BIG VISION, BUT DON'T JUST DREAM. TAKE A STEP.

Julie Barbera

Step Outside the Box

Have you ever felt limited by your own beliefs? You may have heard that mindset is key. You may even understand that what you think about yourself becomes your reality. But if you hope to change, you must first take action.

Think of your world as a great big box. The size of your box determines how much room you have to move and grow. While you may feel limited by the monotony of daily life, you pride yourself in having ventured to the furthest corners on every side. You have even peeked through tiny cracks and crevasses. Although the unknown is exciting, it's far too comfortable where you are to step outside.

True change is on the inside where outside influences lose the power to control you. But the impact of that change is only felt when you allow yourself to be stretched. While you may seek comfort, growth is limited by the familiar. If you hope to examine life beyond the four walls of your box, you must be willing to step outside of your comfort zone.

If a desire to change is stronger than fear of change, you will find the courage to take a step. Step into what you are meant to do, and you will become all that you are called to be. Mindset is key. What you think about yourself becomes your reality. Believe that you can and you will.

IF YOU ARE READY TO STEP INTO YOUR POTENTIAL,
BE PREPARED TO STEP OUTSIDE YOUR COMFORT ZONE.

Julie Barbera

Make a Way

Will you make a way or let discouragement get in your way? Frustration may set in when things don't go as expected. A lack of support from others may make it hard to stay the course. Despite circumstances, you are determined to make a way where there seems to be none.

If others didn't lay a clear foundation, they contributed in other ways. Maybe they taught valuable lessons that you will need for the journey. Perhaps you learned from their mistakes. Whatever the case, you are responsible for your future. And you have what it takes.

Imagine that you are ready to lay the foundation for a road in the middle of a desolate area. There is absolutely nothing for miles. Although you wonder if anyone will ever drive on the road, you recognize the area's potential. After all, it's relatively close to a larger city.

It's going to take months to clear the land and lay the groundwork for a new road. But you counted the cost, and you are sure that you have what it takes to finish the project.

Months go by, and you are discouraged by a lack of progress. The road is longer than you imagined. You set an initial timeline. You knew it would take months, but you still want to see results. Deep inside, you want to believe that your investment in time, money and effort will pay off.

The project is in full force, and you hit a fork in the road.

Unplanned expenses came into the picture when the engineers found an unexpected problem. You accounted for the expected, but you didn't plan for the unexpected. Now you are faced with a challenging decision. Do you forge ahead with the plan, or do you forfeit your investment and cancel the project altogether?

Canceling the project may be tempting. But you think about those who will be affected if you give up. Many have long commutes on dangerous roads. Easier access to the city will change their lives for the better. You have spoken with those living in the area, and they are excited about the project.

Purpose and vision prompt you to continue with the plan. Although you have to find a way to get extra capital, there is too much at stake to quit. A greater investment now will reap tremendous rewards in the future. And you decide that the additional expenditure on your part is worth the risk.

Think of your aspirations as paving the way for yourself, your family and generations to come. The road may be longer than you anticipated, and others may not be as supportive as you would like. Setbacks and detours may occur along the way.

Lay the groundwork for a vision that goes beyond yourself. You will have the determination to press forward when things don't quite go as planned. Unexpected challenges may tempt you to give up, but don't give in. You have what it takes.

If life takes you down a rough road, hold on tight. You will get through the ride stronger than before.

MAKE A WAY WHERE THERE SEEMS TO BE NO WAY.
DON'T GO DOWN A BEATEN PATH.
PURSUE PURPOSE. PAVE YOUR OWN PATH.

Julie Barbera

Dreams in Bloom

Visualize a beautiful garden growing in your backyard. Bright flowers are planted all around, and different species decorate the ground. Bushes are strategically positioned. A large tree is placed in the center. Small from the start, growth can be slow. It takes time to fully grow.

Colors change as seasons change, and growth happens along the way. Plants with deeper roots take longer to bloom. Stability gives them the strength to stay.

Progress happens naturally. Cheerful seeds are scattered around every day. Patience helps when the results are slow. Colorful flowers help to brighten the way.

Think of your mind as a garden. What you focus on daily takes root. If you sprinkle seeds of positivity all around, negativity loses power over your thoughts. If weeds of worry and doubt try to spread, remove them right away. When left unaddressed, they will stunt your growth. They will only get in your way.

Fill your garden with seeds of faith. Water your flowers regularly, and make room for them to grow. In the same way, make space for positivity in your life. Water your dreams daily. Watch as they begin to bloom.

PLANT SEEDS. DON'T WORRY IF THE RESULTS ARE SLOW.
BE PATIENT. IT TAKES TIME FOR DREAMS TO GROW.

Julie Barbera

Lenses of Grace

I magine that it's that time of year again. You have to go to the eye doctor for your yearly exam. If you are like me, you hope that your vision improved. At the very least, you hope that it didn't get worse.

The doctor does an exam, and you find out that you need to adjust your prescription. You are nearsighted. This allows you to see clearly when objects are up close. The new lenses will help with your long distance vision. Reading is also a challenge, so the doctor hands you an order for bifocals.

Confused with the diagnosis, you decide to hold off on reading glasses. Then, you change your mind. It would be valuable to be able to see small print again, so you walk out with two pairs of glasses.

We all see the world through different lenses. Much of what we perceive is shaped by our experiences. Even so, we can choose to change our perspective.

Your views of yourself, the world and others are highly dependent on the lenses that you put on. Glasses of judgment cloud the view. You may need to lay them on the stand and replace them with lenses of grace.

If you look at yourself or others too closely, it's likely that you will recognize every single flaw. Placing a magnifying glass on any problem makes it appear more significant. The closer you look, the more likely you are to notice imperfections.

While it's only necessary to go to the eye doctor once a year, it's helpful to adjust your life vision daily. You may even need to change your view several times a day. When you correct your thinking regularly, this allows you to see through clearer lenses.

The next time you are tempted to pick up bifocals to magnify a problem, set them aside. Take off the glasses of judgment, and put on lenses of grace. Look for the positive, even if it's hard to see. Accept differences. See the world differently.

GLASSES OF JUDGMENT CLOUD THE VIEW.
LAY THEM ON THE STAND.
REPLACE THEM WITH LENSES OF GRACE.
MAKE THE WORLD A BETTER PLACE.

Julie Barbera

The Unfinished Masterpiece

At the end of my *Cracked Mirror, Clear Reflection* writing journey, my thirteen-year-old son Sebastian ran up to me with an inspiring message. Perhaps he knew I needed some encouragement. Whatever the case, I was enlightened.

He said, "Whenever an artist is painting a picture, it never starts out perfectly. There are asymmetrical blobs of blue, green and orange paint. As you watch, you ask yourself, *How will this create a beautiful landscape?* The final product begins to unfold. As time goes on, you see how every blob of paint turned what was once an empty canvas into a masterpiece."

Sebastian is a very talented artist. He can relate to the process involved in creating a work of art. His accuracy, creativity and attention to detail are to be admired. But I am even more impressed with his understanding of this profound concept.

The canvas of our lives is colored with many shades of blue, green and orange. At times, tones of gray and black block the view. Although we may want to see the end result, this would make it even harder to start.

While the picture may be cloudy, it's life's gray moments that mold and shape us. Lovely streaks are added as the story unfolds. Every painting is perfect in its own unique way. Experiences have made us who we are today.

Life is the canvas. Tints of gray may cover bright tones trying to come through. Be patient with the process. The reason will one day be clear. The work is unfinished, and the story is incomplete. In the end, the result is a masterpiece.

LIFE IS THE STORY. GOD IS THE AUTHOR.
VISION GAVE LIFE TO DREAMS.
ALTHOUGH MY MANUSCRIPT WAS INCOMPLETE,
MY ACCOUNT WAS WRITTEN IN TIME.

Julie Barbera

Hidden Treasure

Visualize walking down the beach. Grains of sand line the shore. There are so many that it's impossible to count them all. In search of a treasure, you pick up seashells and place them in a bucket.

Although you have taken this route many times before, today you hoped to find something more. Many shells were far too familiar. They were like tiny specks compared to the vast open sea. Significant yet insignificant at the same time, they merely blended into the scene. Treasures were right before your eyes, yet you overlooked gems searching for pearls.

Gifts and talents that come naturally to you may seem simple. This may cause you to assume that others experience the same ease. In turn, you may view them as insignificant.

While they may be effortless for you, this doesn't make them unimportant. These gifts have been given to you by grace. It isn't your role to determine their value. It's your responsibility to take what you have been given and make the most of it.

TREASURES ARE RIGHT BEFORE OUR EYES,
YET MANY MISS GEMS SEARCHING FOR
PEARLS AT THE BOTTOM OF THE SEA.

Julie Barbera

Raise the Bar

Imagine that you are running through an obstacle course. You have many challenges to overcome along the way. Some prompt you to stoop down, while others demand that you reach high. All require that you calculate risk and make quick decisions with ease.

Midway through the competition, you hit a big hurdle. To make it to the next level, you have to crawl under a barrier and raise the bar. Then, you have to find your way out of a small, contained space in an attempt to make it to the final stretch. You are taken back by this obstacle, as you didn't train for it. You are determined to stand out, so you refocus your mind to push through a mental block.

Now parallel this with life. At times, it can feel like an obstacle course. You have to find your way around hurdles as you adjust and adapt to changing circumstances. You may even feel like you are stuck under a barrier trying to push your way out of a small, contained space. The ultimate goal is to make it to the next level.

Mindset is critical in competition and in daily life. If you lower your standards to match your situation, you won't have the determination to rise above your circumstances to reach your potential. An ability to refocus your mind will enable you to push through challenges and come out on top.

NEVER LOWER YOUR STANDARDS TO FIT IN.
ALWAYS RAISE THE BAR, AND YOU WILL STAND OUT.

Julie Barbera

Stand Tall

What do you do when conditions are against you? You can either lower your expectations to match your situation, or you can rise above your circumstances to reach your potential. The choice is yours.

My eleven-year-old son, Deangelo, recently inspired me through his words of wisdom. I was getting hit by challenges in all directions. Perhaps he sensed this and wanted to encourage me not to give up. He said, "Mommy, when all hope is gone, that's when miracles happen."

At that moment, I had a choice. I could allow challenges to stop me, or get right back up and wait for my miracle. I chose the latter.

Amid trying times, the simplest things in life can be a struggle. It may feel like hard times will last forever. Even so, you have control over how you respond to them. What you do or don't do is your responsibility. The sooner you accept this, the quicker you will take action. And the sooner your life will change for the better.

Life throws curveballs. Learn to handle them with grace. If you can adapt and adjust, you will always stay in the game.

It can be a challenge to go against the grain. But when life pushes you down, take a stand.

DON'T LOWER YOUR STANDARDS TO MATCH YOUR SITUATION.
RISE ABOVE YOUR CIRCUMSTANCES TO REACH YOUR POTENTIAL.

Julie Barbera

The Keys to Success

I magine that you are walking down a long hallway. You have no idea which key fits into which door or which door to try. The only thing you know is that opportunity could be on the other side, and any key in hand could be the right one.

Although the possibilities are endless, real success is hard to find. How do you figure out which key to use and which door is right?

Your first task is to determine which keys to focus on and which to leave behind. The wall is lined with many, and you have to select those that you feel will open the most doors. Nothing is guaranteed, but some are more promising than others. Several open only one, while others unlock many.

The selection of keys is quite extensive: consistency, dedication, determination, persistence and purpose to name a few. While others are shinier and more attractive, the brightest keys don't necessarily open the most doors. So, you decide to leave those behind.

Keys in hand, you try to open as many doors as possible. Opportunity is all around. A right mindset is what you need. If you find the right door, you are confident that you have what it takes to succeed.

Uncertainty and doubt creep in with every attempt, but one thing is sure. Success is on the other side. Consistency, determination and persistence prompt you to try every door. Although several doors open, they aren't necessarily the right ones. Dedication, hope and positivity inspire you to keep going. Faith, focus and purpose remind you of the reasons why.

OPPORTUNITY IS EVERYWHERE. MINDSET IS KEY.
IF THE RIGHT DOOR OPENS, MAKE SURE YOU HAVE THE KEY.
IF YOU TRY EVERY KEY, YOU WILL EVENTUALLY
FIND ONE THAT OPENS THE RIGHT DOOR.

Julie Barbera

Greener Pastures

As the end of a season approaches, you may be looking back on what you have accomplished. Whether you have achieved a lot or a little, it's time to set new goals for the days ahead. Perhaps you have even contemplated making a significant change. I imagine that the thought has crossed your mind, *Is the grass greener on the other side?*

Life is full of rainy and sunny days. As seasons shift, you may be forced to change. Other times, you may choose change and allow it to transform you for the better. Whatever the case, you can walk through life with a positive attitude of expectation.

How do you know when it's time for a transition? The decision is yours to make. Whether you stay put or decide to make a move, accept that things aren't always going to turn out perfectly.

Maybe you have watered and fertilized your grass, but it's still a dry mess. You may have taken it a step further by hiring a company to come over to assess it. Despite your best efforts to stick with what you know, you may need to cut your losses and accept this as an opportunity to grow.

While you may need to stick it out and go through dry seasons in life, don't be afraid to step into something new. While change is inevitable, it isn't always easy. There is a chance you will step into what you thought were greener pastures only to encounter dry patches along the way. Whatever the case, you have to be willing to step out to find out.

When faced with a difficult decision, the right attitude is a choice. Grow where you are planted, but be open to transition. Rather than make drastic moves, think things through. But don't be so afraid to make mistakes that you fail to follow through.

Change is a part of life. In fact, it's the only way to grow. With the right attitude, the grass can be greener on either side.

GROWTH WILL STRETCH YOU. STRETCH WITH YOUR GOALS.
LEARN AS YOU GROW. STEP INTO YOUR POTENTIAL.

Julie Barbera

Grow Where You Are Planted

As your current projects wind down, you may be thinking about turning over a new leaf. Maybe you want to establish a healthier lifestyle, change your career or start a business. Whatever you hope to accomplish, you are ready for a fresh start.

This may or may not be the first time that you have set such goals. If you are like some, your previous hopes turned into nothing more than high aspirations. You find yourself in the same dry spot year after year. You start with new ideas, but your green leaf quickly turns brown. How do you make this a season of new beginnings?

In thinking about a leaf, it doesn't grow overnight. And the tree from which it originates goes through many stages of growth. The same tree that soaks in rays from the sun stands through countless storms.

When things don't go your way, you have a choice. You can resist and wither, or you can accept it as an opportunity to grow. Ironically, a tree doesn't have the option to leave. It's forced to stand through rain and shine. It has no choice but to grow where it's planted.

Perhaps something needs to change inside of you to make this your time of new beginnings. Reflecting on the tree, it has to make the best of its circumstances. While it goes through seasons, change may not be visible to others. Over the years, it builds strength to stand as it grows taller and establishes deeper roots.

The next time you are thinking about making a quick move, think of the tree. Small, gradual changes may need to take place for real transformation to occur. Personal development may not always be evident to others. Maybe, just maybe, you need to grow where you are planted. As you build a strong core, growth will happen naturally. And you will find the courage to branch out and embrace new beginnings.

COURAGEOUS ENDINGS START WITH SMALL BEGINNINGS.
PLANT SEEDS OF FAITH. WATCH THEM GROW.

Julie Barbera

Turn Over Your New Leaf

What if the leaves were to say *I refuse to change*? They might not transition from shades of green to red, orange and yellow. Maybe they would fail to fall from the trees. They may not be willing to share branches with neighboring flowers and leaves.

Life involves transition. Nature reminds us that nothing in life remains the same. Leaves pass through seasons just as we do.

While there is beauty in transformation, there is also resistance. Every stage of life involves uncertainty and risk. Even the calmest of periods is made up of rainy and sunny days. If we hope to grow, we have to be willing to embrace change.

Colors change just like the seasons. We color our lives when we allow change to change us for the positive. A desire to grow and branch out may call our name, yet the fear of the unknown tempts us to stay in place. We say we want a new start, but we don't want to change. We want life to be different while we remain the same.

The next time you are tempted to stay put when it's time for a transition, think of the leaf. It comes from a tree, and that tree grows where it's planted. Growth is gradual, and change happens naturally. Although its colors change in season, it doesn't fight the process. It flourishes and grows beside fellow leaves. At times, it withers and falls while staying close to its tree. Other times, it branches out or flies away with the breeze.

That leaf has something important to teach us. Grow where you are planted. Change in season. Be open to sharing a branch. Blow with the wind, or wither if you must. But above all else, be willing to branch out and take a chance.

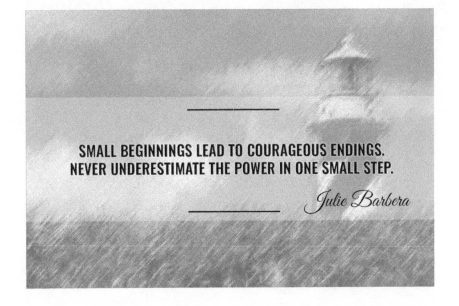

SMALL BEGINNINGS LEAD TO COURAGEOUS ENDINGS.
NEVER UNDERESTIMATE THE POWER IN ONE SMALL STEP.

Julie Barbera

About the Author

Julie Barbera is a life coach and the president of Inspireu2Action. It is her mission to help you to find balance, to become the most authentic version of yourself and to break through to your potential. This passion comes from finding a purpose in her life.

Writing *Cracked Mirror, Clear Reflection* gave Julie the confidence to step out. After years of struggling with an illusion of whom and what she should be, clear reflections in her cracked mirror gave her the courage to take a chance.

God gave Julie the gift of language. Self-taught in four languages beyond English, her goal is to use this gift to impact as many lives as possible. Julie is on a journey to do what she loves, love what she does and live with purpose. She resides in Florida with her husband German and two young sons, Sebastian and Deangelo.

Contact Julie Barbera for coaching services at:
juliebarbera@inspireu2action.com

Inspireu2Action Inc
Boca Raton, Florida

Visit her website: www.inspireu2action.com
Follow her blog: inspireu2action.wordpress.com
Twitter, Facebook, Instagram and Pinterest: @inspireu2action

Newsletter: inspireu2action.com/motivation-in-your-inbox

INSPIRE U2 ACTION
----- BREAKTHROUGH TO YOUR POTENTIAL -----

CPSIA information can be obtained
at www.ICGtesting.com
Printed in the USA
FSHW022358180819
61171FS

9 781733 955003